The COR Method

A Therapy of Evolution and Change

Claudia Miraglia

The COR Method
A Therapy of Evolution and Change

First Edition: 2022

ISBN: 9781524318390
ISBN eBook: 9781524328368

© of the text:
   Claudia Miraglia

© Layout, design and production of this editio: 2022 EBL

Editorial Coordination:
   Ana Caufman
   Priscila Abecasis

All rights reserved. No part of this publication may be reproduced, distributed, or transmitted in any form or by any means, including photocopying, recording, or other electronic or mechanical methods, without the prior written permission of the Publisher.

*To my parents, siblings and nephews and nieces;
they have been a fundamental part of my growth.*

*To my life teachers, for the blessing of
having found them in my path.*

To my patients, for all they teach me.

*And to you, my readers, hoping that the experiences
you find in this book can accompany you in your
challenges. May each word fill your searching soul...*

Table of Contents

Disclaimer 9
Introduction 11
Foreword 15
Chapter 1. From My Own Experience 19
Chapter 2. The COR Method: Dynamic and Tailored 29
    Illuminating the Dark Side to Undo the Conflict 30
    Putting Distance in Time and Space 33
Chapter 3. A Therapy of Evolution and Change 35
    Accepting and Embodying Change 36
    Whoever Comes to Therapy is Healthy 38
    Listening to the Body's Message 40
    Gestalt Therapy 10 40
    Therapeutic Conversations to Understand, Heal and Move Forward 43
    Meditation for the Development of the Self 45
    Patient Independence 46
Chapter 4. A Life to Ascend and Transcend 49
    Courage: Key to the Awakening of Consciousness 51
    Changing Perception: Increasing the Level 54
    Why Do We Assume The Role of Victim? 55

Chapter 5. Better Viewed from Afar: Therapeutic-Spiritual Retreats 59
    Mid-morning Retreats 60
    Therapeutic Travel 62
    The Salcantay Pass to Machu Picchu 63
    India: Poor, Opulent and Sacred 68
    The Southernmost Part of the Planet 71
    Individual Travel and Retreats 72

Chapter 6. Connecting with the Feminine 77
    Sasha: Recovering Herself 79
    The Absent Mother 87
    The Feminine in Man 91

Chapter 7. Why Me? When Tragedy Bursts into Our Lives 97
    The Pain That Awakens Us 99
    Oriana and the Perfect Life 100
    I Feel Blessed 102
    Claudia's Therapy 104
    Lorenzo: from "Why Me" to Unlimited Awareness 106
    Sonia and the Rebirth 111

Chapter 8. Self-esteem and Loss: the Persistence of Life 121
    Margarita: the Feeling of Not Being Deserved 125
    Roberto: the Anxiety of the Unwanted Child 129
    Brigitte: the Value of Being Authentic 133
    Fernando: Success as a Facade 137
    Elisa: the White Sheep. When the Family Doesn't Help 142

Chapter 9. Non-consciousness of Illness 149
    Deny and Hide: Nothing Happens... 152

Chapter 10. The COR Method and the Challenges of the 21st Century 159

Notes 167

References 173

Disclaimer

This book is based on the experience of the author throughout her extensive therapeutic practice. To protect the identity and privacy of the patients who agreed to the use of their testimonies, their names, contexts and circumstances have been disguised. As the author makes no specific mention of individuals or situations in any part of this book, no personal or intimate data has been disclosed that would infringe the privacy of any individual or family.

This publication is intended to provide valuable information to the reader, but it is *not* a substitute for direct expert assistance. If such assistance is required, a competent, mental health professional should be consulted.

Introduction

Since I started writing this book in 2018, there have been many changes that have occurred in the planet, in my country, in my family and in my own life; so much so that my team and I have found it necessary to adjust our agendas and update the information we used when we started. I make this statement, fully aware that this condition of permanent change in which we live, is precisely the premise on which I have built the COR Method, which is a therapy of evolution and change, and, of course, the title and motivation for this book.

As I write this introductory note, I have just returned from a therapeutic trip I made with a young English patient who lives in Ecuador. The trip started in Italy and we traveled through different cities between Norway and Germany. It was a trip expressly conceived without exhaustive planning or confirmed itineraries. The idea was to move among realities — such as geographies and lodgings — in flexible and uncertain times, allowing space for any random situation. We wanted to observe how we make ourselves vulnerable in the moments of uncertainty that befall us. For example, when traveling in these times of pandemic, we have been asked to comply with a series of requirements that vary from one place to another, making us subject to permanent tension. And so we traced our routes among the most beautiful landscapes, encountering all kinds of people, most of them kind, cooperative and respectful. The result could not have been more nourishing and encouraging. The world is not quite done; it has to be done over every day.

What will the reader find in this book? First of all, my life experiences and my training process as a therapist and coach. Someone who studies, analyzes and learns every day whatever is necessary to understand the universes of people who come for help; who ask to speak and be heard; who need to find solutions to their problems and learn to live in a world of uncertainties. The purpose of this self-presentation is to serve as a preamble to talk about **The COR Method: A therapy of evolution and change.** It is a system of therapeutic resources based on different methodologies such as craniosacral therapy, Gestalt therapy, meditation, yoga, retreats and workshops. All of them have been tested by me, and I apply them with full awareness and with full agreement from my patients, keeping in mind what is most appropriate for them, given their nature and life circumstances.

A fundamental part of this book is the testimonies of my patients, who with complete generosity, detachment and freedom share their stories of suffering and redemption. We have changed their names and contexts to protect their identities. To them, my deep and utter gratitude for being an endless source of inspiration and for trusting me, which stimulates me and commits me to be better every day.

I have counted on the editorial coordination of two professionals and friends, Ana Caufman and Priscila Abecasis. We have developed a dynamic of meetings in which we shared our lives and their natural changes and ups and downs. In the end, we achieved a work team in which each paragraph, each testimony, each story in this book transformed us, moved us and has led us to expand our visions of life.

By making my project, the COR Method, known, I wish to share the experiences I have accumulated during more than thirty years of therapeutic work. I have had the good fortune to accompany numerous people, many of whom appear in these pages sharing their life experiences, with the desire that these may serve to help others who are going through similar circumstances. I have learned so much from each patient I have seen and helped to alleviate their suffering. In a miraculous way, we are immersed in a continuous and inexhaustible movement of giving and receiving.

I would like to draw attention to the increasing importance that should be given to mental health. The confinement to which a large part of the world's population has undergone and the crisis caused by the pandemic have exacerbated many of the existing problems, making them more visible. This is now observable in people in public life, such as famous artists who cancel tours due to stress or elite athletes who withdraw from an Olympic competition after admitting that they suffer from depression. Thanks to these courageous statements, we hope that mental health will no longer be a shameful topic to talk about, or one to keep silent about, or to keep as a secret for fear of stigma. The WHO claims that by 2030, the leading cause of disability will be mental health problems, overtaking cancer and cardiovascular disease. I would like this book to encourage lots of people to dare to ask for help, not to resign themselves to living a life on anxiolytics, sleeping pills or stimulants. To find the courage to recognize that we are vulnerable and that our frailties do not have to confine us to a life of loneliness, isolation or suffering; the courage to decide to take charge of our lives, to give them the meaning and fulfillment we deserve.

To me, the COR (Spanish abbreviation of *corazón y coraje*, heart and courage) Method means living every moment with honesty, commitment, joy and deep love for my fellow humans.

Foreword

It is a pleasure and a true honor for me to write this foreword to Claudia Miraglia's work, where she presents the COR Method, a set of psychotherapeutic approaches and techniques for help, self-knowledge, emotional and spiritual growth.

Reading the work that Claudia offers us, defined by her as her life's project, is, to a certain extent, a healing process in itself, since it is impossible not to identify with many of the personal experiences of suffering, change and transformation masterfully described here. Undoubtedly, she shows us her Chironian experience, from the first chapter to the last, and describes in a courageous and open way her whole life experience, the raw material for the empathy and compassion that she puts into practice in her approach to human suffering. Chiron is a centaur of Greek mythology, the son of Cronus and Philyra, with a human head and torso, and the body of a horse. And his tragic story of abandonment and wounds, both of body and soul, teaches us, first of all, human vulnerability and, then, how through these universal experiences we can acquire expertise and wisdom to open ourselves to the suffering of others, trying to heal our own wounds. He thus becomes the "wounded healer", the archetype of all those who dedicate themselves to walking the path of healing, both individually and for others.

My relationship with Claudia has developed in the professional sphere, allowing me to evaluate and indicate, if necessary, the use of drugs, especially in the initial stages of the therapeutic process in some of her patients — a "patient" being any person who suffers and asks for help. In the comprehensive approach that Claudia describes and practices, she clearly understands that pharmacological help is sometimes necessary: it is clear that anguish, depression, insomnia, etc., can initially be relieved with a drug, which allows for a more effective psychotherapeutic approach. This is similar to what happens with physical pain.

The essence of psychotherapy is the relationship that is established between the person who suffers and asks for help (patient) and another who has the capacity and the intention to offer that help (therapist). There are multiple psychotherapeutic approaches and techniques, from very rigid ones, in which the patient has to adapt to the method, to more flexible ones, which adapt to what the person requires and what helps them at any given moment. From her extensive and continuous training and experience, Claudia offers us through The COR (Spanish abbreviation of *corazón y coraje*, heart and courage), a "tailored" process that offers her patients, after a detailed, objective, sensitive and intuitive evaluation, what they need at that moment to relieve their suffering so that they can enter the path of self-knowledge and realization as human beings. Self-sabotage, self-esteem, awakening to other levels of consciousness and meditation are the pillars of her psychotherapeutic work. Referring to the system of hierarchies described by Hawkins in his map of consciousness, and after in-depth interviews, Claudia initially orients herself objectively to the degree of consciousness in which her patient is. Her training in Gestalt, knowledge of psychodynamics and cognitive therapy techniques, as well as her extensive training in craniosacral therapy, are deployed as therapeutic tools for the person to achieve and remain in inner peace. Likewise, workshops, individual and group therapeutic journeys, always with meditation as an aspirational habit, accompany patients in the "transition to self-awareness of their conflicts and to realize the wear and tear of being stuck in them". A desirable amalgamation of eastern and western methods and techniques is put into practice with this process; a need that Jung emphasized in many of his writings and lectures.

Through the description of particular cases, we can delve into the details, results and difficulties that this hard process implies, and in this way, we are shown how it is actually applied in practice. Again, it is impossible not to identify with the processes exposed in these cases, which results in a real, worthwhile adventure. Emotions and afflictive feelings, unions, separations, grief and tragedies are part of our lives.

Finally, this book comes at a time when humanity is going through a global crisis in mental health and suffering, in parallel to the SARS-CoV-2 pandemic and the isolation that it has entailed with all its consequences. Techniques such as *online* therapy, which, to a certain extent, were incorporated into teaching and healthcare, were already being used by Claudia. In her words: "it has allowed me to continue with my activity without having to incorporate significant changes or adaptations to my work and study routine". This has given her greater flexibility to carry out her schedule and care for her patients, wherever they are.

I would like to end this prologue with these wise words that have come up to my mind as I have been reading this work, and which are attributed to Gautama Buddha, more than 2500 years ago: "Pain is inevitable, but suffering is optional".

May you enjoy reading this work as much as I did.

Ernesto Rodriguez Carrillo[*]

---

[*] Internist and psychiatrist. Professor at the Luis Razetti School of Medicine, Universidad Central de Venezuela. Former Head of the Psychiatry Department of the University Hospital of Caracas (Venezuela).

Chapter 1
From My Own Experience

No one ever told me the story of my early years. I relived it in several craniosacral therapies that I underwent as part of my training at the Upledger Institute in Florida (USA)[1]. These were very complex sessions called *clinical applications*. One of them was a therapy in which five people *(Multiple Hands Therapy)* were manipulating me from the skull to the end of the spinal cord, as well as the lower extremities. We started at ten o'clock in the morning and sometimes finished at two o'clock in the morning the next day, since when a process was opened, it could not be stopped. I had previously taken about fifty craniosacral therapies as a patient, so all my channels of communication had been opened, particularly the area of the thorax and neck — with its seventeen muscles — where the heart connects to the mind. In one of those sessions, lying on the stretcher, I felt a very deep pain in my chest. This, as well as other types of *significant detectors,* such as REM and craniosacral rhythm stopping, is part of the dialogue between patient and therapist. I felt fear and saw darkness. I remember that they began guiding me towards that darkness, and we discovered that it was located in the womb. There, a dialogue took place following the Gestalt technique: "Where are you, what is going on?" "Everything I see is dark, I feel heartbeats. I feel a very strong, unbearable pain in my chest". My body turned around and I was face down. Both the person leading the session and the practitioners accompanied this movement with their hands. I remained calm in that position;

the couch felt like my mother's lap. Later I understood that the pain was not mine, but my mother's. The feeling that emerged in that moment was like my mother's pain; it was one of fear, of not wanting to be born. If life was pain, I did not want to live. I recognized through that experience that the pain was very strong. It was an organic response to the information that was emerging. At that moment I was aware that the bond of love with my mother encouraged me to be born, but that was also when I decided that I would not have children. The session lasted for four hours. The blood vessels in my eyes burst. And then I spent a month in fibrillation, unable to work.

In researching what had happened to me, I came across studies that preceded this type of body therapy, particularly those of Wilhem Reich[2], a psychiatrist, psychoanalyst and collaborator of Sigmund Freud, who maintained that a person's psyche and the voluntary musculature of the body are equivalent. Reich considered that muscular contractures were the product of psychological blockages. In his therapies, he resorted to massage, hugging or stretching, to provoke the release of emotions in his patients. For Reich, to touch the body was to touch the unconscious. That is where our experiences are. That is where information emerges.

When talking later with my father about this session, to validate if what had emerged from the unconscious as an experience was true and had not been invented by my mind, he told me that when my mother was pregnant with me, her mother got sick with cancer. My grandmother lived in Acarigua and my parents lived with me in Caracas, so my mother had to travel constantly, taking turns with her sisters to take care of her. And so it was until my grandmother died, when I was one year old. My mother left me in Caracas with my father and a caregiver. Every two weeks she would come to see me and hug me desperately, transmitting all her love but also the pain of losing her mother.

In that intense session I realized that, during those first months of my life, I had assumed my mother's trips as abandonment and as a deep bond with her, from her absence and from her pain. The resolution, the unconscious decision I made then, was not to have children. It is what is known as the "illogical and unconscious decisions of childhood".

Modern psychology reveals that an individual makes illogical decisions from zero to six years of age and these are engraved in the mind in such a way that they condition him or her without being aware of it. When working therapeutically, we seek to focus on the individual's experience. This is the beginning of a truly healing, liberating, psychological therapy. Personally, I consider that this moment in which we become observers and witnesses of the expansion of our consciousness, is the true path to spiritual growth.

I am the eldest of four sisters and I know from my parents that I was conceived with much love during their honeymoon in Italy. I only knew the romantic anecdote. That story, where everything was love, has always been present in my life. To a large extent, it has given me a structure that has subsequently allowed me to endure and overcome hard experiences. Delving into my own history has been fundamental in approaching and understanding the processes that patients go through.

As a child, I had my first experiences of contemplation with my grandfather in the cemetery while visiting grandma's grave. We would spend a long time, sitting next to each other in silence, but very connected. At that time, we had to move to his country estate, known as *La Comadre*, after a series of very difficult events that happened in the family: my mother's car accident, which she miraculously survived, and the family's economic meltdown.

Grandfather was a man of vision. The farm had bungalows, a swimming pool, rowboats, fruit trees, deer; he enjoyed long nature walks. Those were foundational years for the person I am today and for the therapeutic work I do with the method I have developed throughout my life.

Despite my young age, the nature of my environment led me to live in a permanent state of contemplation, so it was normal for me to become aware of lots of things. My capacity for perception and my levels of consciousness did not correspond to those of an eight-year-old girl. I cared for my mother, who was practically an invalid after the accident. I took care of my younger sisters and saw to it that the shopping was done. I was very conscious of family values, whereby we all naturally assumed responsibilities together. Although it was a difficult time for the adult members of the family, it was for me an extraordinary and very special experience. In fact, while caring for my mother, I knew that my vocation would be to care for people and serve as an intermediary to alleviate their suffering.

That childhood in solitude, where I was out of phase with the children in the family and at school, where adults solved their problems as best they could, without noticing the abandonment the children might feel, formed in me a very independent, resolute and self-sufficient personality. Unconsciously, I assumed that I was alone in life. Thirty years later, I became aware of how character can become a rigid personality trait and how that character was limiting growth in my life. Members of the same family emphasize different aspects of the same experiences and, therefore, perceptions of the same event are different and remembered in different ways. When they are negative, these *imprints* can limit us and prevent us from living a full and joyful life.

We know that the unconscious registers constructive, auspicious and creative experiences, but also destructive, compulsive and obsessive ones. Consciousness is a great field where seeds of love or fear can grow. Experiences will always leave an incision in the mind, some stronger than others, because the person assigns meaning to that memory. For example, "I am alone in life". These incisions or illogical resolutions, when engraved from a very early age, are reaffirmed over time and become beliefs that can become very powerful. Some of them limit the person so that their learning capacity deteriorates as a result of settling with what they have learned.

I have been blessed to be alone when it has been my turn to experience notable events. Why do I say it is a blessing, when most people see it as a terrible thing to be alone when some significant event happens to them? Because, from childhood, I learned to value those spaces of solitude that allowed me to reflect on my own processes. One of the great anxieties of human beings can be to feel alone when they have to live through difficult situations. But this feeling of loneliness can occur even when one is surrounded by lots of people; it is not the same as the essential solitude that has allowed me to understand events broadly and deeply. Sometimes, feeling alone is a way of victimizing oneself.

When patients come to therapy, they recount what happened and thus obtain another perception, perhaps different, of what they have experienced. This is very important and is key in any therapy. If at the moment when something happens to us, instead of avoiding it or running away from it, we stay there and become aware of how we feel, we could transform what happens through a new interpretation.

It is important for the person to know the part of his or her history that could explain much of his or her current situation. Many patients do not even know why they come to therapy. They come to solve specific problems without understanding that everything in their lives is intimately linked and connected to a reality that needs to be addressed in order to treat it. They would like to solve their crises immediately and isolate them from everything else that has been their life history.

It is rare for someone to come in search for personal growth. There is always some pressing problem that needs to be solved. The immediate usually does not allow us to see beyond or inside the person. Sometimes it is a matter of simple ignorance. For most people, it is fear that prevents them from delving into a painful and unresolved past.

It is necessary, then, to develop in patients the necessary courage to allow accessing their own history, to find the source of their own knowledge and the possible answers to their suffering. It is precisely at this point where my work begins: I help them to go deep into their inner self: only there can change take place, a true transformation that will bring liberation, healing and happiness.

The pandemic declared in March 2020 became a sort of accelerator of our processes. It not only confronted us with the fear of death, but also placed us in a scenario where all our certainties were crumbling like sand castles. It led us to rethink our way of life, our way of working, our way of relating to each other and finally reminded us how fragile and vulnerable we are.

There is no therapeutic technique I apply to patients that I have not gone through myself. I have experienced them all and I know how far it is possible to go with them. It has been a long journey; years of study and training, of many readings and conversations, of meditation and healing trips, all of which have been linked by hard work to achieve my own spiritual growth. There have also been many years of developing sensitivity, a fine intuition, to quickly understand people's sufferings and how to assist them. In order to help others, it is necessary to achieve one's own health.

I think that the most important thing in my training is to have built a flexible structure, which has allowed me to arrive at what I call the COR Method. From a professional rigidity that would have pigeonholed me in one or another school, it would have been more difficult to maintain that spirit of openness towards the new or unconventional.

Today, we know much more about neuroplasticity, a term that refers to the ability of brain cells to establish new and different connections to create, in turn, new responses to the environment. This, of course, generates a considerable investment of energy by the organism, which, however, is designed to save energy. Therefore, once certain neuronal connections have been developed, the human brain will prefer to issue responses automatically and not generate new ones with the consequent energy expenditure that this implies. Fortunately, human intelligence can reverse these processes. Otherwise, we would be condemned to behave permanently in a repetitive, compulsive, and sometimes even destructive way, in the case of negative patterns. The brain's capacity to transform, change and adapt is intimately linked to the evolutionary process of the human being.

When I speak of evolution, I am not referring to the Darwinian concept of the survival of the fittest. Rather, I lean toward the recent statements of Professor Yuval Harari[3] on how we will face the future, which will require "more emotional intelligence and mental stability". I use the postulates of Howard Gardner[4] on multiple intelligences, or Daniel Goleman[5] on emotional intelligence. All of them appeal to the different intelligences as a potential resource to be developed in order to heal, to grow spiritually and, in short, to promote, based on the sum of more conscious individualities, societies that are more free and just.

I define myself as a therapist of evolution and change. The therapies I use aim to make the patient evolve and accept change as an unavoidable and necessary aspect of his or her life. This is what we also know as evolutionary intelligence: to learn while we are learning. We are all immersed in a process of constant transformation. The human race has not concluded its evolutionary process and we don't know where it will take us as a species. This therapy seeks that the individual delves into his or her inner self, and with deep self-knowledge, begin a true spiritual path of transcendence and fulfillment.

Part of the COR Method is focused on working the psychological mind to reinforce the "ego structure" of a patient. This structure may neutralize the anxiety produced by the conflict between actual conditions, and impulses and prohibitions. It intends to reset the psychic balance of the patient, since without a strong ego structure it is not advisable to begin spiritual work. It is important to be aware of the psychological aspects that limit them; otherwise, there is a risk of falling into pathological behaviors, such as delusions or hallucinations.

My personal history, so far, does not portray disruptive events, as, unfortunately, has happened to many people I know, including many of my patients. I did not live through a war or a natural catastrophe. I did not have a terrible upbringing; on the contrary, I have always been surrounded by the love of my parents, my siblings and my partner of more than twenty years. Perhaps it is precisely within this normality where life's "normal" traumas and problems became more evident. I decided to overcome them through intense, personal work of healing and spiritual growth. And, in that decision, I also included everyone around me and anyone who approached me for help.

As I write this book, I have decided to end my marriage to an intelligent man, with a great vital force, whom I loved very much and with whom I shared important and profound experiences that made me grow and, in some way, get to where I am today. It has been an important decision that comes with the awareness of a lag in the individual growth of the couple. I also emigrated from my country of birth and now move between several European cities. The positive part of the pandemic was the opportunity to reconnect with my paternal lineage in a small village of my ancestors in southern Italy.

I am going through tough family situations, such as the aging of my parents and the health problems that come with it. I am also affected by the planetary uncertainty in which we are all immersed because of the COVID-19 pandemic and the transition to a new century with all the challenges that this implies. What is my place in life? Which path should I take? Do I really have the necessary resources to face this great change? Will I still be doing tomorrow what I do today?

Chapter 2
The COR Method: Dynamic and Tailored

The COR Method is a system of therapeutic encounters through which the person initiates a process of self-inquiry that will allow becoming aware of the conflicts and obstacles that prevent developing the maximum expression as a human being, as well as to connect with the meaning of their own existence.

When a person comes for help, the first thing to do is to schedule a series of at least three sessions, either online or in person. The dynamics of online therapy and face-to-face therapy have different routes, although the goal is the same: to lead patients to discover how they face the obstacles that do not allow moving forward and that are the cause of suffering.

Through these meetings, we can identify if the person meets the conditions to continue with the COR Method. In that case, we define a joint strategy, choosing the most appropriate therapies, according to their expectations, which may range from the resolution of the problem that brought them to therapy to delving into their deepest personal aspects. Occasionally, situations arise in which it is necessary to refer the person to the group of professionals I receive support from, so that the patient can be assisted from a clinical perspective, in addition to the psychological and spiritual ones.

In these three sessions we try to induce a deep relaxation in order to bring out current emotions, which are most probably superficial, but conceal the deeper and more significant ones.

The key is to get the person to relax the nervous system with guided meditations or craniosacral therapy sessions. If the person is physically present and agrees to do it, the latter provides vital information that emerges almost instantaneously.

The method continues with a psychological agreement between the person and the therapist, committing to delve deeper and move forward. The method will then acquire creative dynamics that seek to confront the patient's present reality so that, from there, they can regain their power and strength in order to provide more spontaneous and intelligent answers to that reality.

The next phase of the COR Method consists of recognizing or determining at what level this process is taking place in the person: in his mind, in his body or spiritually. From there, a work strategy is elaborated together with the person, depending on his or her conditions and intrinsic nature. This work plan, so to speak, may include an intensive individual or group workshop, retreats, therapeutic sessions, trips. All this, of course, is developed with a permanent validation with the patients of their process and, mainly, of their responsibility towards themselves.

Illuminating the Dark Side to Undo the Conflict

Existence precedes essence, according to the postulates of existentialist philosophy. It is understood, then, that the most important consideration for the person is "to be aware that he acts independently and responsibly [...] There is no human nature that determines individuals, but it is their acts that determine who they are, as well as the meaning of their lives [...] The individual is free and fully responsible for his acts".

The above statement, by psychotherapist and Princeton University professor Irvin Yalom[6], also an exponent of existentialist psychology, points out that it is necessary to know that there are conflicting forces within the individual — thoughts, emotions and behaviors — some adaptive, others psychopathological.

We ask ourselves: what produces the conflict? Your shadow. And what is the shadow? The dark side in your psyche. It is the aspects that the individual has denied, has rejected and has hidden, but which can be projected onto others. In the language of psychoanalysis, the shadow, or that which produces the conflict, refers to that repressed part of the unconscious, the origin of our neuroses. The work of resolving this conflict consists in freeing the individual from repression and reintegrating this denied aspect of his personality. Resolving these conflicts brings great benefits, because by doing so, a great liberation of energy is achieved that could be used to develop our creative side. Keeping those aspects repressed, hidden or camouflaged, requires a considerable expenditure of energy that would be useful to work on our growth and transformation. Here's a graphic example: let's suppose that the energy needed for our transformation process is equivalent to 600 euros, which we have available in a bank account. Moving to the next step costs us 800 euros. The problem is that we also have another 400 euros pent up or blocked. If we could only manage to release 200 euros of those 400 blocked euros, it would be possible for us to reach the necessary sum required to move to another level of growth and transformation.

A person with a fear of flying in an airplane, who suffers from panic attacks, consumes significant energy trying to calm down, to conceal this in front of his co-workers, and to create excuses. If this conflict could be resolved, the energy released would allow this person to expand his or her radius of action, to reach more people, to open up to a greater number of opportunities.

The conflict of abused women, in many cases, does not cease to be so because some of them legitimately raise their voices, as, for example, in the #MeToo movement. If this "me too" comes from a feeling of shame, very common in this type of victim, then true liberation does not occur. However, for abused persons, to denounce and demand justice is the first step to overcome shame. But we know that it is not always easy.

Part of the therapy that I apply in these cases is the exploration of the different polarities in the individual: pride/shame; malice/naivety. The world of polarities is infinite and the more it is explored, the more the consciousness expands and the greater the integration of the aspects that may be in conflict. Hence, the individual has a greater acceptance of himself and, therefore, of others. At this point, the judgments that we persistently make about others disappear.

There are many ways to work on conflicts or shadows. The person seeks the support of a qualified therapist or participates in seminars, courses and group therapy sessions, which are very effective, since it is usually on another person that we project our unintegrated polarity. The COR Method provides this space.

At every stage of human development, the psyche suffers wounds that leave scars that may be encapsulated. A wounded person may be in permanent closure or contraction to cope with an existence that hurts irremediably. Each wound and each contraction is the origin of a type of conflict or neurosis. Some of them, those which are psychological in nature, can produce projections or avoidances; and others, of a psychopathological type, can give rise to schizophrenia, bipolarity, etc.

There is a very common case of anger repression that occurs when a small child gets angry with his mother. This feeling of anger causes the child to feel threatened, since he knows that his survival depends on the bond of love with his mother, so he unconsciously decides to dissociate or repress his anger. By denying anger, the child is alienated from his own emotions and feelings. This translates as follows: "I'm furious with my mother, but showing my rage threatens my emotional connection to her, as well as my needs for food, safety, comfort, and survival." Many times, that repressed anger is projected on oneself or on people who have no idea of the problem which caused that anger towards them. And this goes on because the child, and later the adult, does not acknowledge his or her own rage since it is so often put aside.

Putting Distance in Time and Space

A requirement that the COR Method proposes to the patient is to withdraw, to learn to create a space of intimacy with oneself in one's daily life for a certain period of time. Whether in a face-to-face or online session with me, during a craniosacral therapy, meditation or conscious reading session, the person must necessarily withdraw from their daily environment in order to immerse themselves deeply and make contact with themselves.

Within the proposal to distance oneself from the daily routine, there is a wide range of possibilities, from the twenty minutes that meditation can last, to an hour of therapy, to a trip to a remote place outside their comfort zone. Later we will see in detail some experiences that have given successful results.

From the retreats and deepening workshops, the person begins to feel more capable of managing his or her own life or any situation he or she is going through. They become aware of the need to find their own space to take control of their own destiny.

In the following chapters, we will see some examples that illustrate how the different therapies that make up the COR Method have been applied. We highlight different models, such as craniosacral therapy, Gestalt therapy, meditations, *Kundalini yoga*, retreats, workshops and trips. None of them are exclusive; all of them are complementary.

The ultimate goal of the COR Method, which is dynamic and tailored to each individual, is to help the person to achieve and remain in inner peace. It proposes a transition towards self-awareness of their conflicts, to become aware of the wear and tear of being stuck in them. The aim is to bring the person out of this state of paralysis in order to take control and power over themselves. In short, the goal is to induce in the individual the awareness that it is possible to achieve a full, creative and harmonious existence.

The COR Method can be more than a therapeutic option; it depends on the person, and whether she or he decides to take a look at the infinite number of windows and paths that open up when taking this offer of a life full of meaning.

Chapter 3
A Therapy of Evolution and Change

The therapy room smells like peace. Soft music and a faint scent of flowers are forcing me to give in. I came in tense, with sagging shoulders and teeth aching from so much clenching. The noise outside does not interfere with the silence in the room. There, it seems that the world has stopped and is inviting you to do the same with your inner treadmill.

There are armchairs, rugs and a couch where I lie down. The therapist speaks to me slowly, almost whispering. I lie on my back and immediately adjust my body to the ergonomics of the cushion. The therapist holds my feet on each side, firmly but gently. There the action begins. I close my eyes and my heart begins to beat rapidly. I'm afraid of that tachycardia, but I want to keep going. My mind doesn't stop. And neither does my heart. Both in a wild race to see which one can do more. The therapist says nothing. After a while, she places her hands on the center of my chest and presses. My heart slows down. My mind does too. The therapist asks me, "What is it inside you that causes you so much pain?" "Time hurts," I tell her. Time that goes by so fast; it takes the children from home and takes away the love, the skills, the lushness. I'm sorry I didn't know this sooner. I would have enjoyed it more. Five years ago, my daughters left. They got married and left the country, far away. Five years ago, I had surgery; my womb and ovaries were removed. I was left empty. The decline began. I am afraid of getting sick.

This is the testimony of Patricia, a woman in her sixties. Everything seems to be going well in her life. She has a well-constituted family: her husband, her daughters, her grandchildren. However, she does not sleep at night; she has a problem of wear on her teeth and a very annoying gastric reflux. Patricia's mother is very elderly and she has to take care of her. She works in an important position for a cosmetics company. It doesn't pay very well, but she likes the environment.

For the first time in craniosacral therapy, she became aware that the operation she underwent due to fibroma and constant hemorrhages meant a mutilation for her, the loss of her femininity, of her youth. It coincided with the departure of her daughters. For Patricia everything was fine. Everything was logical and natural. She raised her daughters to be independent and she succeeded. The operation, an advisable and necessary health issue, also went ahead. Patricia was never, until then, aware of the pain that both losses had caused her.

Accepting and Embodying Change

"Change" is a word that today we need to understand, accept and embody into our lives. The losses we suffer involve changes that we generally find difficult to assimilate. Resisting change has been one of the most common and also one of the most limiting attitudes. Although we know that, right from our conception, we are constantly transforming because the world we live in changes every second, and life itself is dynamic and mobile. We wonder why every change in our lives seems a crisis; why we tend to be static; why it is so hard for us to accept these transformations as something natural and positive.

Fanaticisms, says the writer Amos Oz[7], originate and settle in those who refuse to change for fear of being considered traitors.

"A traitor, I think, is someone who changes in the eyes of those who don't want to change and can't conceive change even though they always want to change you."

We do not move forward because we are comfortable or we fear change, of leaving our routines, our beliefs and convictions behind. Yet it is necessary to learn to change, to accept change as something natural and desirable in our lives. Change is inescapable and it is necessary to heal, to grow and to evolve. Let us remember that evolutionary intelligence consists of learning while learning occurs.

Much is said about the urgent need for a paradigm shift in order to begin to understand today's world. That should seem obvious; so why is it so hard for us? We are faced with more diseases without cures, more violence, wars, climate change. In short, more questions and fewer answers; less certainty and more uncertainty.

Countless scientists and philosophers have been proposing new models to study reality, that have led us to understand that the universe is a network of interconnected events, and that matter and spirit are complementary concepts. These findings have forced scientists to approach eastern philosophy and thought in search of answers. And many have realized that in this world of interrelationships, everything we do and what we think forms energy fields capable of conditioning the very nature of life. Prayer, meditation and collective fasting are millenary practices that westerners are now discovering as great panaceas for all human suffering.

In her book, *The Field*, journalist Lynne McTaggart[8], through a series of interviews with a group of scientists from different disciplines, has compiled the results of daring experiments with phenomena such as thought synchronies, telepathy, remote observation, memory and consciousness.

McTaggart reflects:

> We have more power than we realize to heal ourselves, our loved ones and even our communities. Each one of us possesses the ability, and together we have great collective power, to improve our lot in life. In every way, we hold our lives in our own hands.

It is precisely from this position of openness and freedom that, throughout my professional career, I have developed the COR Method: a system of therapeutic resources through which I help the people who come to me not only to overcome a crisis or to cure a specific problem; my goal is to accompany them to achieve their greatest potential as human beings. I called it COR, because those are the first three letters of the Spanish words *corazón* (heart) and *coraje* (courage), as both words define the essence of the COR Method, which is my life project.

Whoever Comes to Therapy is Healthy

There are societies in which going to therapy is not very common. Most people do not consider it unless they have a serious crisis that forces them to seek help. In schools, universities and companies there are counselors and psychologists who provide help in their fields. Even so, it is difficult to find people who individually seek the help of therapy to delve deeply into their histories, to heal their wounds, to grow as human beings. We often hear the expression "I don't believe in psychologists". In fact, most insurance companies do not consider the mind, let alone the soul, as a subject to be covered by their policies.

Sometimes suffering becomes chronic and becomes part of our reality. We learn to live with the pain, we settle, until something detonates some inner fiber that aggravates the problem. The crises that happen to us can open doors to paths of healing and spiritual expansion. But it takes a minimum of health to realize that something is not right. People who decide to seek help have a level of consciousness that allow them to question, even to confront, situations that represent a conflict. These are the people who have the "courage" to review their lives.

Through the COR Method we try to identify the obstacle that the individual has and then the level of consciousness in which they find themselves. These can vary from one area of the person's life to another. I can have high levels of consciousness in my professional life and very low levels in my personal life or vice versa. In low levels of consciousness, the person is victimized; there is always something or someone to blame. The breaking point comes when the individual acquires the courage to stop being a victim[9].

That is why this method of work and research is phenomenological, as it may be considered more suitable for dealing with psychological cases. When acting as a therapist, I am not an objective observer, because I do not place myself outside the facts, but within them, and those facts will also transform me. Everything happens at a given moment and will instantly change. In the same session, the levels of perception of both the patient and the therapist change. That is why it is not possible to speak of a measurable observation as in the patterns of classical science. Each person and his or her relationship with therapy and the facilitator enters into an exchange of emotions, information and perceptions that represent a unique and unrepeatable experience.

Generally, I try to examine from within the facts, review the contents of the consciousness and determine whether such contents are real, ideal or imaginary.

The first thing, undoubtedly, is to listen to the patient, understand his or her reality and establish a connection where empathy and trust arise to initiate a therapeutic dynamic. If the patient agrees, we then begin with sessions of craniosacral therapy or meditation to get the nervous system to relax.

Listening to the Body's Message

Craniosacral therapy, developed by the osteopath John Upledger in the 1970s, is based on the subtle manipulation of the area from the skull to the sacrum and throughout the spinal cord to perceive the fluctuations of the cerebrospinal fluid and its possible impact on physical and mental ailments. After a long training process, the certified therapist, by palpating different areas of the patient's body, is able to recognize a rhythm and intensity that reveal states of crisis, suffering or trauma of the patient. During palpation, emotions come to the surface; the patient may cry, feel fear, anguish, pain, palpitations or pleasure, or simply fall asleep. The patient may then become aware of the event that generated the wound that marked a milestone in his or her history.

Gestalt Therapy[10]

In the therapy room, six people are gathered in a group session. All participants enter into the process. The therapist notices how some exhibit anxious behavior. Many are attentive, others unfocused. The nervousness of one of them,

Anabella, causes a great disturbance in the group. Anabella is visibly uncomfortable and wants to flee the room. She has a tendency to distrust everything and everyone. She's very shy, and seems reserved in an unfamiliar environment. She's afraid of not receiving approval from those around her. She's forty-two, married and has two children, fourteen and ten. Anabella has her own financial consulting firm. She leads a team of six people.

The "empty chair" is one of the tools of Gestalt therapy, which allows individuals to recognize in what way they make contact or not with their experiences. It consists of two chairs facing each other. In one, Anabella sits as she presents herself to the world: a person who always shows herself as strong, self-confident; and in the opposite chair sits the other Anabella, the child, unprotected and vulnerable. The therapist asks the adult Anabella to choose from the group someone who makes her uncomfortable. She selects Roberto, thirty-four, tall and robust, who is sitting with his arms crossed.

"Why him?" asks the therapist.

> "Because of his serious attitude, he seems to be judging me. It makes me feel uncomfortable, I feel a pressure in my chest."

Anabella, the child, begins to cry, situating herself on the day her dad left home. She was seven when her mom told her that he was gone forever. He left and she never saw him again. A great pain prevents her from speaking.

> **Therapist:** How do you feel when you see Anabella, the child, crying? What would you say to her at this moment?
> **Anabella, the adult:** Don't be sad. Daddy is not here, but I am here to take care of you.

Therapist: Where is your mother? Why don't you share your pain with her?

Anabella, the child: She is locked up in her own pain. I can't rely on her.

Therapist: What do you want to say to adult Anabella?

Anabella, the child: That I admire her very much and that I thank her for taking care of me all this time.

The empty chair tool is intended to reproduce an encounter or situation, and thus bring to consciousness a certain emotional state to promote a different interpretation of the facts that allows the closure of unfinished processes.

Often, patients reject it because it pinpoints authority: mom and dad, and they are not yet ready for that contact. Gestalt therapy opens the capacity to establish contact with situations and people and allows us to distinguish the way we avoid establishing those contacts. We are constantly interpreting and arguing reality. For example, we see a tree and notice that it has grown, but we did not experience it. Gestalt therapy makes it easier to talk about something, once we have experienced it. When someone comes in and tells me that he is very violent and fights with everyone, we have to identify where that repressed anger is. Gestalt therapy uses the empty chair technique with the intention that the person, first of all, becomes aware of his division and can confront that alienated, unknown part of himself in order to integrate it, and thus be able to reorganize his perception. The opposite is always in front of one, and Gestalt therapy integrates it so that it stops projecting outwards. The psyche is not even aware that this possibility exists.

As a therapist, I seek to integrate the patient's intelligence as a resource to improve relationships. And when we talk about intelligence, I'm referring to psychologist Howard Gardner's conception of the multiplicity of intelligences, which are understood more as capacities or skills that the individual must develop than as an unalterable genetic condition. In accordance with this dynamic and creative approach, I work with the patient to unveil his or her particular and specific intelligence potential in order to put it to the service of a better relationship with his or her reality and, ultimately, with his or her healing.

With Gestalt therapy, open situations are reviewed and rearranged. In therapy, as in life, processes are often more important than content. Gestalt therapy allows us to close unfinished situations; situations that keep repeating themselves with differing content.

Therapeutic Conversations to Understand, Heal and Move Forward

Many people, when they come to therapy, are not aware of their problem, they are trapped in an emotion that does not allow them to see or realize what is happening to them.

When people begin to become aware of their situation, I start therapeutic conversation sessions, for which I use empathic listening, which allows us to focus and move forward. Empathic listening involves total attention to achieve a deep connection with the person. Focusing, indeed, is a Gestalt therapy technique that I use as part of therapeutic conversations. To focus is to identify and put the magnifying glass on some area that has been neglected, repressed, ignored and avoided and that has been conditioning the individual's life without their being aware of it.

In philosophy, this method of interaction between two people is known as maieutic and involves a methodical dialogue so that the questioned interlocutor can discover the truths for himself.

When working with craniosacral therapy, a process of sensitization is initiated with the patient that opens up the possibilities for a therapeutic dialogue or conversation.

A young thirty-eight-year-old patient with a well-established family and a successful professional career suffers from panic attacks every time she knows she has to travel by plane. At first, she was deeply unaware of her process and wanted to resolve her problem with immediacy. I asked her to participate in meditation/body therapy. She was not even aware of the repression in her body. She could barely breathe. After that session, we continued with online therapy and her story began to emerge: an emasculating father who physically punished her, so she would lock herself in a bathroom to get away from him. This was how the patient spent much of her childhood, dealing with her emotions in a bathroom. There, she, listening to music, recomposed her stability herself, but she was unable to overcome the fear she felt. It was necessary to do deep focusing work with her and show her where this fear was coming from and why it had not been overcome.

Many fears are experienced during childhood. During its development, the child gradually faces them as part of its maturity process. This process had not been completed in this young girl.

If the patient is prone to projection or avoidance, the therapeutic conversation will not be of much use. It is preferable to use another technique to sensitize them to their own situation.

Therapeutic conversation through maieutics and focusing delves into the individual's problems. These conversations should emerge from a bodily sensation of the patient and not from a rational process of his or her mind, by which the person tends to fall into anecdotal conversations that contribute little or nothing to the therapeutic process. The patient must be sufficiently sensitized to become aware of his or her process.

The therapeutic conversation with Ileana was very helpful. She was very aware of her reality of living in a dysfunctional family; her mother had a psychotic condition with depression, and her father had severed all relationships with his parents and siblings. Ileana's maturity, despite being only a thirteen-year-old teenager, helped a lot in making her aware of her role within such a complex and toxic family structure without her falling into victimization.

Therapeutic conversations lead the patient to recognize and take responsibility for a given situation or relationship: to stop looking for someone to blame, to stop complaining and to understand that they must satisfy their own needs or rethink them, and not wait for another person to come and satisfy them.

Meditation for the Development of the Self

Once the individual reaches a higher level of awareness and commitment to his or her own process, I incorporate into my method meditation techniques learned from masters in India, Portugal and the United States, in order to improve the individual's capacity for attention, perception and cognition. This "understanding" through realizations and insights can activate very deep processes in the psyche that lead the patient to true liberation from the causes of his or her suffering.

I began to incorporate meditation into the COR Method when it became a fundamental part of my life routine. After having done a good deal of body therapy and psychological therapy, I began to travel to India, so I embarked on a process in the unconscious where I could see my ego with greater depth and clarity: the lack of compassion, the lack of self-knowledge, the lack of gratitude, the superficiality. In short, my immaturity. These experiences caused me a great impact and I decided to train with Hindu spiritual masters and then share this information with people who would be hard-pressed to travel to India to undergo this type of process. I was also able to see how important and powerful collective meditations are to raise the vibration of the participants.

There is a moment when the individual who has begun to deepen his sensitization process and has become aware of himself and his environment, shows the potential to delve even deeper, far beyond what can be achieved in a therapy room.

Once the person has satisfied his primary needs for nourishment, communication, expression, to be loved, to be accepted, to be fulfilled, to be esteemed, etc., the imperious need for self-development and to transcend arises. This need does not emerge from the psychological mind, but from the spiritual mind. At this point, I invite the person to integrate meditation and self-inquiry as daily routines in his or her life.

In my many searches, I have found countless western scientists and thinkers who have incorporated meditation techniques into psychotherapy. At Harvard Medical School, for example, they offer meditation workshops for students. Also of note is an interesting volume, *Mindfulness and Psychotherapy*, edited by Harvard psychologists Christopher K. Germer, Ronald D. Siegel and Paul R. Fulton, who, together with a group of prominent researchers from various American universities, show interesting results from their meditation experiences with their patients.

Patient Independence

Meditation within the COR Method, as a tool to train the mind to learn how to consciously observe thoughts, emotions, patterns, stories and the sensory world, is a way to make the patient independent from what could become an eternalized therapy. When I see that the patient has reached a certain maturity in his process, I suggest spacing out the therapy sessions. The idea is that meditation replaces therapy and that the patient comes, in principle, every two weeks or once a month and can exchange experiences, realizations or insights with the therapist. In this way, the patient is freed from therapeutic dependence, without losing the direction of his or her own progress.

Some people find it easier than others to get into the habit of meditation. On my YouTube channel I have posted a fairly simple technique for users to practice twenty minutes, every day for a minimum of eight months.[*]

It basically consists of contemplating the thoughts of the mind that come and go, like a hotel doorman who lets guests in and out, but does not follow them to their rooms or follow them into the street.

The mind, in order not to wander, needs some direction. In most people with excessive emotional content, the mind lacks the ability to concentrate, to focus. The focus in meditation is to contemplate and not to be carried away by an emotion, sensation or thought. Through meditation it is possible to be in the present time and, from that state, to train the mind in a subtle way in the observation of the processes in the different planes. At first, the individual will achieve this for only a few minutes, but the goal is to practice at least twenty minutes a day so that they can open more spaces without resistance.

After contemplating thoughts, we move on to observe emotions. Emotions are energy and many times we make it very dense. The only way for us to consume that energy, whether it is anger or pain, is to stay in that experience or, as I call it, "consume the coal."

---

[*] https://www.youtube.com/watch?v=k4b6lGpB0Dg&t=22s

Obviously, to get this far, the patient has already been able to identify and internalize his or her emotions and knows that there is no reason to avoid or deny them; that he does not have to judge himself for feeling anger, pain, fear; that the thoughts that sustain those emotions are not necessarily real.

After having contemplated thoughts and emotions, meditation seeks to open the heart of the practitioner, bringing him or her to a state of non-resistance, through total acceptance of all that is. The highest expression of self-acceptance is love, and there is nothing more healing than vibrating in unconditional love. In fact, one of the greatest sources of human conflict and suffering is non-acceptance, the failure to accept ourselves, others and life as it is.

Some people are reluctant to meditate, contemplate or observe. Their minds are very agitated and contain obsessive thoughts. This is a typical characteristic of fear. Let us remember that all the therapeutic work of self-knowledge can produce a lot of fear in the individual. Fear of discovering what is in him.

Chapter 4
A Life to Ascend and Transcend

Once a deep connection is established with the patient through therapies that allow them to relax and share their problems, we move on to the second stage of the COR Method, which consists of identifying the individual's state of consciousness. This is crucial in the way the therapeutic dynamics will develop. It is not the same to begin a physical or psychological healing process with a person who is sensitized to the facts and circumstances of his own life as with a person who is unaware of the responsibility he has for the way he thinks, feels and relates to his environment.

Why is consciousness so important? Because for all the species that possess it, consciousness is the basic instrument of survival: the ability to be aware of the environment in some way, at some level, and to orient action accordingly. I use consciousness here in its primary meaning: the state of being aware of some aspect of reality.[11]

Psychoanalytic studies develop the concept of the unconscious to define the space in the mind where our experiences remain hidden and are not recorded in memory, but that condition the personality and behavior of each person. Consciousness is, therefore, that space where we bring such experiences to process them and turn them into a recognizable part of our lives.

With the emergence of new research technologies, other studies on consciousness have appeared in the field of neuroscience, based on experiments on the behavior of the nervous system and the brain. We are witnessing, then, a new conception of mental processes that acquire materiality, insofar as their study is objective and follows the scientific method.

However, it is very interesting that, in spite of scientific advances and the need to ground ourselves more and more in the specifics of the problems that afflict human beings, the postulates of eastern philosophies, today adapted and disseminated in all scientific and academic circles in the West, have re-emerged with greater urgency.

Studies in human consciousness have been since their beginning complex and difficult to grasp for those who do not understand the subject. Fortunately, they have evolved, bringing new contributions to the knowledge of the psyche and its potential for expansion and adaptation to provide the human being with greater happiness and fulfillment.

Today, it is widely recognized that any type of illness or ailment, be it physical, mental or spiritual in nature, finds its maximum capacity for recovery when the physical, psychological and spiritual are treated simultaneously and with the same importance. This comprehensive approach increases the possibilities of a positive response from our organism.

To better understand all this, I have taken as a reference the theory of scales of consciousness, developed by the prominent American psychiatrist, philosopher, writer and researcher of consciousness, David R. Hawkins[12], whose theory is compiled, in works such as *Healing and Recovery* or *Transcending the Levels of Consciousness*, among others.

After several decades of study and research with hundreds of patients, including himself, Hawkins developed a scale of the feelings and emotions that a person can experience in different circumstances. It is a method that attempts to give a stratified numerical value to these "energy fields" from lower to higher. It is a valuable attempt to make objective those feelings and emotions that make up human nature. According to this scale, everything that happens to us existentially can be placed on one level or another and, by becoming aware of it, it becomes possible to overcome it, and to ascend and transcend it. When we refer to everything, we speak of life, of its changes; of being healthy or sick; of our relationships with our parents, with our children, with the people around us; with what causes us suffering or joy. In short, with what it means to live in the present, without forgetting the past and looking to the future.

In the following chapters, we will refer to this methodology to establish the relationship between body, mind and spirit, which is crucial to treat anything related to the healing of the individual. The application of this map is very useful for the treatment of a wide variety of human problems ranging from stress, alcoholism, disease and depression, to fears and phobias, just to name a few.

Courage: Key to the Awakening of Consciousness

"What can I do with the life I have been given?", asks Edith Eger,[13] a Hungarian-born American psychologist and Holocaust survivor. It is the most important question we can ask ourselves at any given moment. And that is the way to recognize that we are alive not through victimhood, drama or suffering, but from the capacity we have to live to the fullest the life we have been given. It is necessary to reach the level of consciousness that provides us the courage to ask ourselves this question.

The levels of consciousness depend on our vision of life is and the emotion that accompanies it. According to Hawkins, in levels below 200 the individual has an existence of suffering; above this level, we progressively experience the state of "truth".

Anything below the 200 level is not compatible with life, since it does not sustain it. In other words, fields below the 200 level potentiate illness, victimhood, helplessness and defenselessness, while those above this level are compatible with healing. Placing oneself above the level of courage (200) marks a milestone in the evolution of a person since at this point a transformational change is generated in his or her life. Courage is understood here not only as a virtue of bravery and strength, but as Brené Brown[14], University of Houston writer and researcher, states, it is "the complete acceptance of our own vulnerability as a way to feel whole." Vulnerability, Brown argues, "is at the core of shame, fear and our struggle for dignity, but it is also where joy, creativity, belonging and love are born." Exposing ourselves to our own vulnerability, accepting imperfection is the beginning of the dissolution of the ego.

But it takes courage to take responsibility for our lives and acknowledge our vulnerability; to expose ourselves to a society that requires us to be strong and successful. To be vulnerable means to understand that within our own unique human condition we are perfect in our imperfection. Because being strong, beautiful, intelligent and successful are just advertising posters, labels that make us believe that they are the only access to happiness.

We can be strong by recognizing that we are afraid to travel by plane or to speak in public. We can be beautiful by appreciating the passage of time in our face. We are intelligent when our life manages to have meaning, and we definitely triumph when we are able to expose ourselves with deep honesty before others.

Álex Rovira[15], a Spanish writer and lecturer, maintains that "courage, more than the absence of fear, is the awareness that there is something worth risking ourselves for. Courage is strength at the service of love and conscience [...] Courage allows us to mobilize energies, feelings, emotions and visions so that we can reach beyond our imagination and transcend our own limits. The acts that come from courage raise us above our possibilities and shape our lives."

The enormous spiritual power above the 500 level facilitates recoveries in a way that is inexplicable from a scientific perspective.

All these fields are so powerful that they dominate our perception of reality. According to these energies, we will see our inner world and the world around us. In fact, these fields or levels of consciousness, as Hawkins rightly argues, influence neurotransmitters. From level 200 and above there will be a release of endorphins, which produce pleasurable and happy sensations. Below this level there will be a predominance of adrenaline and animal instinct reactions typical of survival states.

As we continue to ascend in the scale, we can reach, even if only temporarily, the state of pure consciousness, i.e., consciousness itself experienced in the infinite field of energy called consciousness. At this level there is no notion of separation between the self and all that surrounds it. The ego is transcended. There is no identification represented in the "self" and the "other". The "self" transcends the mind and is recognized as consciousness.

As a therapist, one of my goals is to identify the obstacle the person has and the level of consciousness they are in.

These levels are not static, they can vary even in an instant. If you have courage, the capacity for liberation is different, you have more strength. To reach the courage level, one must have vital energy and that is the first thing I try to identify when patients come to my office. When the individual manages to maintain that level of energy, it is less probable that they will lower the level of consciousness.

An exercise I like to do in my workshops is to have people, identify a situation in their lives, in each of these levels, and contemplate their vision of life in each one.

Changing Perception: Increasing the Level

I'm in southern China since the past eight days for an agro-food engineering congress. I had been warned that the season was very bad, due to an atmospheric phenomenon called the monsoon, in which it rains non-stop for three months and you can't see the sky or the sun. I never thought it would be like that, but when I arrived, it was worse than I had imagined. The first few days my spirits were low. It didn't stop raining, it was cloudy, no sun, unbearable traffic, and everything was wet.

After a couple of days, I began to realize that a great sadness was coming out from within me in an inexplicable way. The origin of this melancholy could not only be the weather. At some point, I decided to stop evading and looking for excuses to not observe and experience in depth the suffering I felt. This exercise of contemplation, without judgment, allowed me to transcend what until then had been a repeating pattern in my life, this time triggered by the bad weather. Making contact with that pain dramatically changed my attitude towards the circumstances.

From that experience I realized that, although it was beyond my control to influence the weather, I *did* have the power to consciously intervene in how I responded to it and change the way I perceived it. At that moment I realized that we always have choices. In my case, I either let everything affect me negatively, discourage me, lead me to stay locked up in the hotel, or I could choose to feel gratitude for the blessings that the water also brought. That simple but profound reflection changed my experience in China. I began to feel gratitude for everything, not only for the water, but for having the opportunity to visit that country and expand professionally. I became more productive in my work meetings, more receptive to the possibilities that opened up for me, more energetic, more attentive to details; things started to flow better in every way. I would leave the hotel and give thanks for the water and the rain that filled everything with life, that nourished the plants, that cleansed the environment of pollution.

The eastern philosophy of life, practiced for thousands of years, advises us to accept with gratitude all that life gives us, without judging, without labeling. See the good and the magic around us. There is a world full of possibilities and it is up to us to see it or not.

This experience, shared by Alberto through social networks, illustrates the change that a person who has worked and overcome the obstacles that prevented him from moving forward, can bring about. On his own, he was able to ascend from the level of victim where he was, to the level of courage, to understand that it was up to him to make that journey a successful experience instead of a failure. After several years of committed and sustained work with the COR Method, Alberto has developed an admirable ability to influence his perceptions, face every challenge in his life and overcome it.

Why Do We Assume The Role of Victim?

From birth, the human being establishes a relationship of total dependence on the mother, who nourishes, provides love, comfort and the security of being able to be and remain in the world. Babies cry because they are hungry, or because of a colic, or because they need contact with their parents. Their communication system is a very precarious one to make themselves understood, and only the mother can sense what each tone or timbre of her baby's cry means.

Babies are so dependent on their mothers that it takes them a couple of years to understand that they are different human beings than their mothers, and it is part of the mother's job to achieve, through love, that this process of individualization takes place in harmony. Because separation is not easy, the baby cries when the mother moves away or when she does not carry him. The mother, who suffers when she hears him cry, soon comes to satisfy her little one's demand.

If this process of separation between mother and child does not take place in an emotionally healthy way, manipulation and blame between both may be installed in the relationship. The child becomes the victim of a situation that he understands as "abandonment" and blames the mother. The mother, on her part, becomes the victim of the son's urgent and unsatisfied need.

That child may grow up feeling that the world or life is indebted to him and that if he cries or complains enough, he will be able to get what he wants. The child will soon learn that, by getting his mother to see him as a victim for his lack of attention, he can succeed in exerting some degree of manipulation over her: a vicious circle which, if not broken, can be very damaging.

Being a victim is a way of being that, unfortunately, we observe frequently from early to later ages. It is a way of being in life and in our relationship with the people around us: with our parents and siblings, with our schoolmates, with our relationships, in our jobs. It is a behavior as common as it is pernicious, and sometimes very difficult to identify.

When we settle into victim mode, anyone can be responsible for our suffering or discomfort: my partner, who left the house; the neighbor, who is drilling; my boss, who does not value my work; the government, which does not increase pensions. In short, everything and everyone is working against me. If we take it to extremes, being a victim can turn into a state of paranoia where everything external can potentially, or actively, be perceived as a threat to the individual's safety or survival.

Mrs. Begoña is eighty, and complains bitterly that she is locked in her house every day of the week and doesn't go out anywhere. She has three children. The eldest daughter lives next door and visits her every day. The middle daughter picks her up every Saturday and takes her to the mall or shopping. On Sundays she goes to the park with her youngest son. Her children work and have families to take care of.

In the neighborhood, there is a group of ladies who get together and the mayor's office organizes dances, talks, crafts, musical activities, etc. for them. But Begoña is reluctant to go. She has never really liked socializing. Every day she wakes up with high blood pressure. Her three children are worried and at the same time resigned to the fact that nothing they do or propose will help Begoña feel good. Obviously, she is not aware that her role as a victim generates great distress in her family and, therefore, she is not going to do anything to change that situation. Her eldest daughter, however, is in therapy working on her role in this relationship, so that she can assist her mother without being overwhelmed and without feeling guilty, and thus avoid repeating the victim pattern.

Acting from the level of consciousness of the victim is not the same as actually being in a situation in which we have been in disadvantage, in which we have been physically or emotionally assaulted. Being in the world means that we can be exposed to adversity, to violence, to an accident, to an illness. But as real as this possibility is, it is up to us to keep in mind that, despite our inherent fragility, we also have the infinite power to not let circumstances overwhelm us. Although it is neither obvious nor easy, it is important to identify the pattern of the victim, work on it consciously and reach the level of courage from which we can always overcome and move forward in every challenge that comes our way in life.

In therapy, I consider it fundamental to make individuals aware of the patterns they have followed throughout their lives, which decrease their personal power and turn them into passive subjects, instead of conscious persons with full power and responsibility for everything that happens to them. When the victim is not worked from an individual perspective, the collective becomes equally ill, since a natural derivation of victimhood is its antagonist: the victimizer.

Once we reach the level of consciousness from which we can experience courage, we begin to feel the impulse to change the direction of our lives; we feel the vital energy to decide that we will no longer be victims of anyone or any external circumstance, and it is at that moment when we can delve into our psyche to find our own answers and solutions internally.

Chapter 5
Better Viewed from Afar:
Therapeutic-Spiritual Retreats

We always say that time offers us the necessary distance to better understand the problems and crises that affect us. It changes our perspective and we can even come to see them without the drama or the importance we gave them at the time. Withdrawing, moving away, or isolating ourselves for a period of time: from an instant or an hour to a month, a year or more, can prepare us to become witnesses of our own life.

Separating ourselves from our natural environment for a certain period of time can also bring enormous benefits. Retreats, be they religious, therapeutic, spiritual or business, are a very effective tool to promote this distance from daily life, in order to focus attention on a problem or need, and thus find solutions or new ideas that allow us to move forward.

Since those walks with my grandfather in the cemetery when I was a little girl, I have had many opportunities to be alone with myself and contemplate the world around me with admiration. I have very vivid memories of *La Comadre* farm, paddling on the lake, walking among the mango trees, enraptured by the sound of the water, the smell of the rain-soaked earth, the smell of the ripe fallen fruit. My father was going through a difficult time financially and I remember seeing him walking along the lake to distract himself from his worries. I also remember watching my mother walking with difficulty while recovering from her traffic accident. All these family vicissitudes helped me understand the importance of being in silence. We shared the suffering and worries from a serene silence, without drama, without stridency. Retreating to read, enjoy nature and the silent closeness of my grandfather was a privilege that molded in me one of my most precious virtues as a therapist. Silence and contemplation are practices that allow me to intuit, appreciate and understand what is happening around me.

The practice of retreat dates back to time immemorial. Many eastern and western cultures have established throughout their calendars days of prayer and even fasting to take a break from the daily routine of their lives, lower stress levels, find answers in silence and stillness, improve mindfulness, concentration, optimize performance, or seek the spiritual reconnection so necessary for human beings.

When I was training in Gestalt therapy, we had a ten-day retreat twice a year in a paradisiacal place on the outskirts of Caracas. We started at half past seven in the morning and there were days when we finished at midnight. I experienced very transforming moments during those retreats.

Since then, it has been very clear to me that taking a break from our routines and withdrawing from daily life is of utmost importance to be able to go deeper into ourselves, without the noise of the daily hustle and bustle.

Mid-morning Retreats

I didn't know what I was going for. I didn't even wear the right clothes. We did yoga, meditation, spiritual exercises. It was five hours where I could be with myself. Especially in the world we live in, these retreats of calm and peace are much more appreciated.

I felt a great liberation from my own personal burdens and at the same time, these burdens were replaced by a great deep love for my being.

These testimonies from Ricardo and Mildred show how the mid-morning retreats conceived within the COR Method for healing are increasingly necessary.

The purpose of this activity, which can take place once a week in an appropriate space, is to initiate or create the habit of introspection in people who do not do therapy, either because of prejudice, fear, or because the costs are unaffordable.

The mid-morning retreats provide a space for growth for groups of people whose challenge is — in spite of each bringing different problems, or their processes of self-knowledge being at different levels — to work on a specific issue in their lives that needs attention and to make a resolute commitment to themselves.

The process begins with the sensitization and raising of the levels of consciousness of the group. This is very important because if there are people with guilt or shame consciousness among the members, the rest of the group will move towards their very low levels of consciousness. The same happens at the global level. Then, in order to mobilize participants, questions are proposed depending on the specific theme chosen for each session. For example, if in the retreat we are going to work on personal power, I will ask questions such as "in what kind of situations do I lose my personal power?" and "why am I living someone else's life and not my own?"

Subsequently, we enter into a more psychological stage, in which participants become aware of their state and the possible causes of a problem that afflicts them. Using the previous example, recovering the power that dwells in each one of us goes through acknowledging the excessive self-criticism, fears and insecurities.

The goal, in short, is to create awareness of how necessary it is to work on ourselves, on self-knowledge.

Therapeutic Travel

I developed this space with a great friend who has a lot of experience in group travel to India and other Asian countries. We teamed up to manage small groups and include psychological and spiritual therapy as part of the proposal. After the first trip to India, I clearly saw the importance of considering places like the Salcantay Pass, on the way to Machu Picchu, in Peru, where, in the Peruvian Andes, we reached heights over 4000 meters above sea level, before finally arriving at the mythical Inca citadel with the superb Urubamba River at its feet. Or the Argentinian Patagonia, where the Perito Moreno glacier stands like a fantastic natural wall of ice before the incredulous eyes of visitors. And, of course, the Camino de Santiago, in Spain, one of the world's main pilgrimage routes since the Middle Ages, which is not only visited by Christians, but transcends the religious to become a true spiritual path.

Some of the places I choose are those that I consider to be a challenge for the patient, for the expansion of their world and their consciousness, either because they are culturally opposed to their customs or traditions — as in the case of India, Bhutan, Nepal — or because they represent a physical challenge, which demands a great capacity to adapt to the environment. Experiencing nature through excursions, long walks or hiking in the mountains allows us to become aware of the perfect interconnection between everything that exists; to become aware of and marvel at the creation of the universe.

The therapeutic trips have been very successful and have given me great professional and personal satisfaction. I have been able to observe the enormous progress of patients through the group therapies, favored, in addition, by being outside their usual places of reference. Many were discharged after returning from these trips.

The Salcantay Pass to Machu Picchu

Roberta was a patient who had been receiving craniosacral therapy for more than eight years and who found it very difficult to express herself in the therapy room. With her, we traveled to Cuzco, the ancient capital of the Inca Empire, with its archaeological remains and splendid Spanish colonial architecture, located over 3300 meters above sea level. This was the scene in which we carried out an intense session that consisted of a group Gestalt therapy. There, Roberta was able to experience total liberation from her role as a perfect woman, who kept her life under a rigorous order at the expense of her own happiness. The dynamics of the therapy was initiated by a member of the group, who was encouraged to share with the others situations or personal experiences that represented a source of suffering and stagnation or blockage in her life. The testimony of Vera, one of her traveling companions, who suffered from alcoholism, triggered in Roberta a feeling of empathy and solidarity that allowed her to open up as never before, neither in therapy sessions nor with her most intimate circle of family and friends.

After listening to Vera, I invited the group members to express how they felt, what the story they were hearing had awakened in them. Roberta then began to recount her own experience, as the wife of an alcoholic and as a mother stripped of her role for fear of confronting male authority. She did so serenely, without any dramatic charge, with admirable honesty and clarity, the product of years of therapy. Roberta was able to feel confident within the group. She no longer had to keep up appearances, nor hide her suffering.

While it is true that not all patients are able or willing to go on a therapeutic journey, getting them out of their comfort zone is a very effective way to move their heartstrings, confront them with their reality and make them see themselves reflected in the different life circumstances of their fellow travelers.

The retreats can be of contemplation, meditation, silence or in workshops, which always include the first options and also a practical component. The workshops can be of ten, twenty or fifty hours, depending on the initially proposed goals. A more advanced stage of these retreats is what we call therapeutic journeys, which can be in groups — in which case the mode of work is focused on the collective, but treating what emerges in the sessions individually. As an example of this I cite group therapeutic journeys to address issues such as femininity or issues such as self-sabotage, victimhood, identity processes, self-esteem, liberation from patterns of suffering and connection with joy and the sacred in our lives. The therapeutic journey designed for a single person is established when the person is not ready or does not feel able to share their process with others.

Another testimony from these therapeutic journeys is that of Hannah, a widowed, forty-three-year-old woman, who had many unresolved childhood fears and insecurities. Physical, psychological and existential fears that were expressed in a great immaturity that did not allow her to move forward in her personal life or to face her new situation: premature and unexpected widowhood.

Hannah was raised in a totally urban environment; she never had contact with nature. The child of overprotective parents, she was never taught to swim, ride a bicycle, skateboard, or any physical activity that posed an accident risk for the little girl. Instead, the child took refuge in board games and studies, so that she developed a great analytical and rational capacity that would later become a very characteristic feature of her personality. Hannah's sensory or bodily awareness as an adult remained practically nil. This was reflected in the first sessions of craniosacral therapy that I gave her when she came to my office and through the therapeutic conversations that we had in the first meetings. It was important to orient the therapy to a process of alignment and balance between mind, body and spirit. Hannah had become a spectator of life and not a protagonist. This was very scary and conflicted with her desire to shine and show herself to the world. It was not an easy job in the beginning, due to over-rationalization and little awareness of her body and physical capabilities. I remember her dismay when I invited her to do the Salcantay Pass; I also remember that day when she used all her courage to take on the challenge and accept the invitation. The therapy began with daily outdoor physical training so that she could activate a process of body sensitization and begin to become actively involved in a more protagonist life, as a previous step to assume herself as a leader or agent of change in her environment.

Hannah: (The night before leaving for the excursion, very upset and crying). I don't understand *what* I'm doing here. I am irresponsible. I am in no physical condition to make this journey. I think the most sensible thing to do would be to wait for you here in Cuzco, do some sightseeing and meet you in

Machu Picchu. I'll arrive by train. That's what I'm going to do. That's my decision.

Therapist: Hannah, you are already here and we are going to travel together, by foot, to the wonderful Machu Picchu. That's what we came here for.

At this point, I used the role of authority as a therapist, which generates confidence in the patient.

Hannah: No, I'm not going. I didn't come here to die. I don't understand why I agreed to come on this trip. I've fallen several times and I've had sprains; I've never camped or slept outdoors in my life. I'm afraid of heights!

Hannah's level of consciousness was fear and this logically affected the rest of the group, who also became aware of their own unexpressed fears but decided to transcend them. It was a very beautiful process of expansion of consciousness.

Therapist: Hannah, we're all in this together. I want you to understand that your decision affects the group. We've been preparing for months to come here. You have trained your body on long hikes in the mountains for more than three months. Do you remember that stick you found in El Avila that you used as a walking stick? You said that would be your amulet to overcome all difficulties. Reaching Machu Picchu through the Salcantay Pass is the dream of everyone in the group. We will not leave you alone. We're here to help each other. This is not only a physical issue, but of spirit, teamwork, communion and enjoyment of nature. Connect with that.

At that moment it was essential not to feed the patient's doubts, but, on the contrary, to help her to break her limiting beliefs and self-sabotaging patterns that prevented her from contacting and enjoying the magic of nature.

Hannah: But *my* parents would never let me go on a field trip like this! It's too dangerous. I'm afraid of dying a tragic death. Falling into a river, down a ravine — I'll be a nuisance to you, believe me, you better go without me!

Therapist: Hannah, *do you* think that after all the wonderful work you've done, victimizing yourself and blaming your parents is going to help you overcome your fears? Who's talking now? The Hannah with a thirst for adventure and discovery who made the decision to come on the trip or the five-year-old Hannah who plays at putting together puzzles, one after another, locked in her house because they won't let her go out to play with friends so she doesn't fall and hurt herself?

At this point, it was important to make her aware of the deep stagnation she was in.

Inviting Hannah on this high-risk, high-performance trip was a crucial part of her therapeutic process. We had had long five- and six-hour workouts on flat and mountain roads. Therefore, I knew Hannah was physically trained. What was paralyzing her were her psychological fears, and I was aware, as a therapist, that these types of episodes would be surfacing throughout the trip. Hannah's trust in me was extremely touching and that made me return that same trust to her at every turn. There were situations where she faced great and complicated challenges. Fear at times paralyzed her, but she had moments of great joy when she could feel proud of her accomplishments as her body and mind responded to the physical challenges. Her ability to marvel at the exuberance and majesty of nature was inspiring. The solidarity and affection of her fellow travelers were very important to her and gave her a lot of security.

The group helped her cross bridges, follow narrow tracks, climb mountains and even to convince a Quechua farmer to lend her his mule so that she could finish climbing the Salcantay before the night fell and the temperature dropped dramatically. The whole group celebrated seeing her appear triumphant on the animal's back. Of course, Hannah had never even ridden a pony in her life. Back in Lima, preparing for our return home, at our closing meeting, Hannah shared with the group her feelings and learnings and said she felt "ten years wiser and ten years younger". The Salcantay Pass was the first of many treks that Hannah continued to make around the world.

India: Poor, Opulent and Sacred

India is perhaps one of the most fascinating places in the world for people and, paradoxically, the one that creates the most resistance in others. It is a tremendous contrast. People who have accompanied me on the deeply spiritual journey that India represents have in one way or another experienced a wonderful transformation in their lives. Not everyone is a candidate, obviously; people with strict religious or cultural conditioning or with an inability to adapt to what is different are usually not very open to this type of experience. In these trips, I look for people to immerse themselves in the culture, but, above all, in the millenary spiritual tradition of that country and for them to experience sacredness as an important aspect that they can integrate into their own beliefs. I have heard people who have made this kind of trip say that they are better Catholics or better Jews. We visit temples, participate in rituals and meditations. They are trips of at least twelve or fifteen days, which implies letting go for a while of routines and obligations that we have in our place of residence, work, and family, and this requires making adjustments and rearrangements in our life agendas.

Marina, who has a large family, is at the head of the family business, founded by her maternal grandfather, which is a leader in the pharmaceutical industry in Costa Rica. Despite her success as a businesswoman, she suffers from the rivalry among her six children. She blames herself for the mistakes she made when they were still small, such as having them too close together and not being able to devote enough time to each one; or the comparisons she constantly made between them; or the demands and requirements that were not in accordance with the different personalities of each one. With her youngest daughter the relationship was even more difficult and conflictive. Marina had decided to accept my invitation to a therapeutic trip to India and one day in the therapy session she told me that she wanted to invite her youngest daughter, Berta, to come with the group.

After several interviews with her daughter, whom I did not know, I decided to incorporate her into the group of travelers. Being a very cultured young woman, she showed interest in the historical sites, in the rich handicrafts, and was always willing to try the typical Indian dishes with great curiosity and enjoyment. However, she flatly refused to participate in the group therapies and meditations scheduled during the trip. I managed to get her to at least be present at the sessions, even if she did not get involved. As a therapist, I was aware that I had to give Berta a lot of space so that she could learn to relate in a different way to the authority I represented at the time.

Berta slowly began to become sensitized to her mother's suffering, which emerged in several group therapies in which I included deep meditation techniques. In one of them, Marina was able to express the feeling of abandonment that had accompanied her since she was a very young child; in another session, she recounted the physical abuse she received from her father, who made no allowance for her being the only girl, and applied the same physical punishment as her brothers. She remembered her mother being helpless and submissive as she watched her husband beat her children mercilessly. She also recalled with bitterness how her mother, Berta's grandmother, spent most of her life engaged in philanthropic work in the hospitals of San José to escape from an unbearable family reality. Berta was surprised and visibly affected. She had never heard her mother talk about her childhood. Even more, she had never seen her mother cry. Marina always kept up appearances and avoided any kind of sentimental outpouring because she did not consider it appropriate. The pain that emerged from Marina would not have been possible or would have been very difficult in any other context. The company of women, who opened their hearts and showed their vulnerability, was very mobilizing for her and her daughter. Something wonderful followed these deeply human and moving sessions. The mother was able to get in touch with her pain and begin to forgive her parents; the daughter, in turn, was able to connect in a previously unsuspected way with her mother. In a single therapeutic exercise of projection through drawing, Berta was able to become aware of the lack of clarity she had regarding her identity as a member of a family in which practically everyone was a stranger to her.

The frustration, resentment, and pain of not being enough, or of not being able to respond to family expectations, dissolved and in their place a beautiful emotional mother-daughter connection emerged, based on love and compassion. It was an important first step to becoming aware of the need to strengthen self-esteem in each of them.

The Southernmost Part of the Planet

As I explained before, not everyone can go to India, the distance together with the costs and one's own limitations can be a difficult obstacle to overcome. Sport and its practice in nature is an extraordinary therapeutic tool and there are many fascinating places in the world to discover. Thus, the idea of an expedition to the Patagonia with a group of women with the clear goal of working on aspects of their femininity, such as facing challenges of loneliness, sensuality in its different stages, fear of old age and their role as women in the family, in society and with themselves.

The majestic environment of the Argentinian Patagonia, at the southern tip of South America, surrounded by mountains and lakes, along with the warm and comfortable facilities where we stayed —with views of Lake Nahuel Huapi and the Perito Moreno glacier, which is an imposing and fantastic presence of the landscape — served as an ideal setting to delve into the processes of this group of brave women committed to their change and evolution.

I sensitized the group so that they would allow themselves to be permeated by this nature that awakened beauty, sensitivity, fecundity, exuberance and serenity.

From there, the group was preparing to go deeper into the discovery of the feminine. I asked them all to play the roles of women from ancient and contemporary history so that they could reflect on the fact of being women in the times in which they lived and highlight the power they exercised in society and the attributes that made them special.

Manuela is a widow who has turned to work to fill her emptiness. An emptiness that, in reality, already existed when her husband, an alcoholic and jealous man, was alive. It is more than likely that Manuela, in order to not attract attention and thus unleash her husband's fury, gave up "being feminine" or the expression of what this meant to her. For some years she hid behind the façade of the general management of an important transnational telecommunications company.

At the beginning of the trip, she assumed the group tasks with a lot of competitiveness, a very typical trait of hers, accustomed as she was to large corporations. Gradually the playfulness took over and a very interesting process of sensitization began. It was very revealing that a person with a tendency to hide or go unnoticed, in those days, took special care of her personal grooming and in the importance she gave to posing in group photos. An almost adolescent joy began to surface in her.

The contact with the majestic nature of the place, the winter and its white tones, created an ideal setting to help us become aware of the natural cycles of change and how they influence our lives; something essential in the processes of women.

Manuela was able to recognize how her early family environment with a very dominant mother marked a submissive personality before authority, from which she could only free herself through professional success, reaching high positions, an authority which, paradoxically, she ceded in her personal life.

Upon returning from that trip, Manuela was able to recognize in herself all those attributes of a woman that allowed her to get back in tune with her nature, strengthen her self-esteem and freely give herself to a relationship of mutual respect, admiration and affection.

Individual Travel and Retreats

These trips are designed for those people who, either because of their agendas, lifestyles or personal processes, have the possibility of doing them individually with the therapist. This is the case of Carlota, a young Mexican woman with a very Nordic mentality. She has been living in Norway for twelve years. After a year of online therapy, we jointly decided that it was necessary to continue the therapy in a face-to-face and intensive way after her divorce and the beginning of a new relationship.

We could say that her first problems in Norway arose from the drastic change of climate. She lived and grew up in Mexico and when she moved to Norway she had to adapt to the lack of sunlight. Carlota also felt vulnerable and even discriminated for being Latina. Her self-esteem was very affected and she may well have suffered from postpartum depression.

However, professionally, she is a solid person and aware of her worth.

On this occasion, Carlota suggested that I go to Norway. She herself organized the whole trip, booked the tickets and the cabins. I don't usually delegate this kind of organization to third parties but, on this occasion, I agreed because of her enormous knowledge of the place and her particular sensitivity towards the natural environment.

She was very eager for me to meet her family and see all their accomplishments. Where they lived, where their daughters were studying. They welcomed me with a great dinner and I felt all the time that Carlota wanted me to meet her new partner, in her new home. It was like a session of gratitude and recognition. The next day we left for the retreat.

In Norway, the people on vacation usually go to cabins where their ancestors used to live; many of them don't have electricity or internet access. There, the great challenge is to disconnect from everything, from comfort, from communications.

Carlota's attitude of total openness was crucial for us to get to the core of her negative pattern.

The place where we went was incredible. It was located in the Lofoten Islands, in the Norwegian Sea, above the Arctic Circle. There we found landscapes of mountains and beaches and the famous fjords, which are sea inlets resulting from the melting of the glaciers; a mythical, breathtaking and extremely healing nature.

We were together in a cabin. We would get up at six in the morning and start working on guided meditation and role work. Carlota could not tolerate being in the same room for two hours or she would go into a state of anxiety. So, we would go for walks, long walks in silence. You could see how her love of nature was part of her stability.

We could work until midnight, since it got dark very late in the summer. Precisely that same light, so longed for and so absent in the winter, was a valuable resource that made the intensely developed therapy work more efficient.

Throughout the journey, we had very challenging experiences that allowed us to discover many negative patterns of self-sabotage inherited from her parents.

The last sessions with Carlota were intensive, because of the dynamics imposed by the place itself and because it was necessary for her to identify and accept those patterns she was denying. We did Gestalt and craniosacral therapy. Carlota acquired key tools to be able to go even deeper in the recognition and acceptance of those patterns that prevented her from reorganizing her life in a more harmonious way.

Personally, this was an experience of love and healing I have rarely experienced. It was wonderful to see Carlota's evolution in her own geographical and family environment. To feel how trust and respect came naturally and, far from affecting the therapeutic relationship, it enhanced it.

The experiences of the groups of people who have made these trips have encouraged me to creatively develop the subsequent ones I organize. The same happens with the retreats and workshops that I devise as I learn from each experience. With each of these distancing practices I review the therapies I apply, evaluate their effectiveness, renew the concepts I have learned, investigate again and come up with other techniques and other possible ways of interacting with the groups. My intention is that the person puts a real or symbolic sea in between their comfort zone. That they undertake a journey not only through a different space, but through their own geography, that they draw their own healing maps and that they travel without straying from their paths towards a full and happy life.

Chapter 6
Connecting with the Feminine

The identity of a person is an issue that has been studied from all possible perspectives: from psychological and cultural to human rights aspects. Assuming the identity that corresponds us as human beings is an issue that has concerned us since ancient times. We are all human, male or female; we have a nationality; we have a religion or a political position; we belong to a cultural group; we like music or sport. We define ourselves from the inside according to our feelings or our sexuality. And from the outside we are defined by how we are seen and where we can be easily and superficially placed.

Although identities are necessary because they give us a basis for situating ourselves in relation to our environment, they are often a limitation because they are not enough to define the complexity of the human being. We can no longer speak of masculine and feminine genders, nor of unique nationalities. The identity that defines us as individuals is part of the process of self-knowledge that we decide to undertake or not. We become aware of who we are, of our reality in the world and in the circumstances in which we live. We then act accordingly and feel fulfilled if we can achieve our goals in accordance with our chosen identity. And on this path of life, we overcome conflicts and difficulties by drawing on the values that identify us. In our first years of existence, having a clearly defined identity is fundamental for the development of a healthy and stable psychology. But as children grow up and become adults, that same identity can be a major obstacle to their evolution.

I am therefore inclined to argue that identity, though necessary, is not a definite aspect of life. Thus, we understand that, basically, we all assume an identity, but it is called to expand in order to enrich the personality of the individual. Spiritual evolution implies a process of dis-identification, of abandoning the positional aspect of a rigid identity that confines the individual to live according to patterns or beliefs that prevent him from developing his intelligence and new responses to the challenges of the changing environment.

We do not share the closed definition that characterizes women based on their sex and in a contrasting and antagonistic manner to the concept of masculinity.

The challenge we face today is to understand personal identity, although we know that this concern was already raised by the Greeks in the famous aphorism "know thyself", which appeared in the 4th-century BC.

We want to approach this topic from the way in which the masculine and the feminine are related, or as the Spanish philosopher and anthropologist Blanca Castilla de Cortázar explains[16]:

> Virtues are human and must be developed by each person, male or female. There is, therefore, no difference between masculinity and femininity. In this sense, Jung discovered that each sex was complementary within itself. Indeed, Jung noticed that the sexes are not only complementary between them, but within each other; and he spoke of each male having his *anima* — his feminine part — and, as a counterpart, each woman her *animus* — her masculine part. In this sense, Ortega y Gasset's comments on *La Gioconda* are interesting, since, in

his opinion, Leonardo did not paint the portrait of a woman, but the feminine part of his own soul. "The more complete, from the point of view of nature, a man and a woman are, the more complementary they are to each other and the deeper the harmony that unites them".

Thanks to the collaboration of some of my patients, who have generously consented to share their experiences of suffering and redemption to help others, I have been able to bring to this book some stories that describe the processes of human beings who decided to make the commitment to transform and evolve.

The COR Method, being a technique based on the phenomenological, does not work according to closed diagnoses, but is based on the change of perception of the individual as a result of the increase of his level of consciousness. This is, undoubtedly, what allows to transcend specific conflicts with which they arrive at the clinic and experience a profound liberation and expansion of the being.

Sasha: Recovering Herself

Sasha is a woman in her fifties, whose parents gave her a stable family nucleus, both materially and emotionally. Being the daughter of immigrants was one of her greatest strengths, as it endowed her with an admirable strength of spirit and ability to overcome challenges.

Sasha spoke very little during the weekly craniosacral therapy sessions she attended for severe migraines that would leave her impaired. I knew little about her: that she held a very responsible position in a private company, but she didn't talk about her current family. Instead, from time to time she allowed herself, lying on the couch, to remember her childhood.

> My greatest affinity was with my father. My mother was the one who took us along the path of duty and etiquette: get up, comb your hair, eat, get dressed, do this, do that... My father was the one who gave us balance. He was a musician; he would have liked to be a doctor, but he couldn't because of the war. He was a very spiritual man and he was my escape valve, when he hugged me or when he became an accomplice in the face of any scolding, any obligation coming from my mother. I always felt more connected to him than to my mother.

We observe how Sasha acquired models of compassion, flexibility and sensitivity from her father rather than from her mother: models that traditionally could be attributed to the feminine. The mother, on the contrary, was the one who imposed discipline and authority.

In general, she recounts an "idealized" childhood, with freedom and good socialization tools. This trait, however, was absent in her adult life, confined to her work environment and to a lot of loneliness.

Her level of consciousness fluctuated between fear and pain, which produced a lot of anxiety and a terrifying vision of life. Work and impersonal relationships were her escape and false refuge. Psychologically, she had developed a withdrawal mechanism as an escape.

Sasha's sense of duty was paramount for her. She was a person with a highly developed superego: the perfect daughter, the perfect student, fully adapted to her parents' wishes. She never rebelled or questioned whether what she was doing was what she really wanted to do.

> I studied Business Administration, but I really wanted to study Social Communication and I got the third best admission

exam, but my father was worried because it was a career in which a lot of time is spent on the street, and for me, my father was a very special person. So, the next day I went to the university and requested the change to please him.

In short, everything seemed to be working according to the patriarchal family's pattern in Sasha's life, but at what point did that seemingly peaceful life cease to be so?

Sasha decided to leave a partner she had had since she was a teenager, with whom she had known selfless and idealistic love, for a man thirteen years her senior who represented security, stability, material progress, rather than romantic love and the uncertainty of growing up with a person of the same age, but without any prospects for the future. A decision made from rationality, perhaps from that pragmatism learned at home, which, however, did not bring her the happiness she longed for in a harmonious home like the one she knew in her childhood and in which she had felt safe and protected.

> My marriage was a very hard experience; the hardest of my life. I had to learn many things that I never saw in my parents' house. I had a movie-type ideal of life, in which everything was rosy, but it wasn't like that. I would set the table and there was no one to tell me how good the food was and, many times, when I got up in the morning, there was not even that person to say good morning to or to have coffee with.

This situation worsened every day and Sasha became so fed up that she no longer even wanted to foster an affectionate atmosphere, convinced that nothing could repair her seriously damaged relationship.

> A year into our marriage, I would say to myself, "Gee, is this what I chose? We shared the same ambition and passion for the job, but there was no love. And I didn't do anything. I kept walking in my individuality and, because I was doing so well at work, I developed a mechanism that allowed me to go on with my life without caring if he came home for dinner or not. I was no longer waiting for him.

The level of consciousness at this stage responded to a deep apathy, which served to hide her despair. Without realizing it, she had given up on being happy.

Sasha's marriage was moving towards failure. The relationship of this couple, once the dazzling stage was over, seemed to reveal that it had only been conceived from interest and not from love. So, it developed as a relationship in which work, ambition and competition were installed in an environment where there should be emotion, tenderness, empathy and affection. But neither of them had reached the level of awareness of courage, which was necessary to get in touch with their emotions and be able to express them to the other.

So Sasha, consciously or unconsciously, decided to develop a pattern of avoidance that would develop into compulsion and addiction to work. The couple decided to have a child as a new "project," but as the child grew older, it only widened the great gap that already separated the marriage. For Sasha, the "child" project was a way to please her husband with the illusion of becoming parents and the hope for a change in their lives; for her husband, it was an escape that would allow him to project all his failed dreams and ambitions. The crisis escalated and numerous surrounding problems further aggravated the situation of an already fragile home, without the capacity to withstand the first storm that human beings, families and businesses will inexorably encounter throughout their existence.

One of the strengths of the COR Method is learning to listen to your inner self. Many times, crises are announced by a mood or body discomfort that we tend to overlook, without stopping to explore its origin. The level of consciousness from which Sasha acted was fear, which generated in her a permanent state of anxiety that led her to retreat into her work. The most common thing in these cases is to evade, hoping that this dissatisfaction or silent pain will disappear by ignoring it. And so, we decide to live our lives until the suffering becomes unbearable. It is then that disease sets in as a response to a body that collapses in the face of stress or pain sustained over time.

Pregnancy and motherhood represented for Sasha a reconnection with her femininity. She looked forward to the birth of her son. During the first months, the child became her priority, so work and professional demands took a back seat. But soon the "child project" ended up being the object of great discord between the couple due to their having very different conceptions regarding the child's upbringing.

> Before Alex was born, it was a shared, beautiful project, but after the birth, our central life project, the only one we shared, that linked us, did not have a single moment of connection. It was exhausting trying to convince my husband of the need to give the child structure, schooling and to have him interact with other children his age. He became so obsessed with him that he would not let anyone, absolutely no one, not even me as his mother, intervene in his upbringing. I gave in so much, and more and more often, that I came to separate myself from lots of important activities for Alex, because the fights with his father were unbearable.

Sasha allowed her husband to take her nine-year-old son to another country to train as a professional tennis player, as she felt that she could not do anything to stop him. Her frustration as a mother was settling in her life and she became convinced that she did not have the tools to fight against the imposition of a husband who didn't take her into account; she assumed a role from the conscience of a victim in a situation in which she declared herself impotent. That is to say, according to Hawkins' scale of consciousness, Sasha was below the 200 level —the critical point—, from which the individual with a mature attitude can take control of his or her life. Thus, she ended up taking refuge in work and her husband in alcohol. The marriage continued to deteriorate.

> I was desperate. I had always been a woman of faith and, in my religion, I found the comfort and strength to go on. One day, on the advice of a colleague at the office, I went to see Claudia. And I started going to therapy on a weekly basis. That was my space of peace, of relaxation, of meeting with myself.

Sasha's severe head and neck pain brought her to my practice. The first thing that emerged in craniosacral therapy was the great pain caused by maternal emotional abandonment. A very battered femininity had to be supported and sustained. The same pattern of submission to an authoritarian mother surfaced and was repeated in her current relationship.

The family settled into apparent functionality. However, with the onset of her husband's alcoholism, he became violent and jealous, to the point that Sasha panicked that at some point he might physically attack her. She felt defeated and knew that nothing could save the relationship; a gap of resentment and distrust separated them.

> We met again, but I must confess that I was very afraid to give in again, and I also felt a lot of resentment. I felt anger towards him for all that I had suffered because of his depression and his aggressiveness. I admit that I did not feel like accompanying him in his recovery process. I did not love him anymore.

The husband began rehabilitation and, although Sasha acknowledged seeing a significant improvement in his character in this stage of sobriety, something had changed in her and it was irreversible.

Sasha's husband relapsed into alcoholism and died tragically in a motorcycle accident, apparently due to drunk driving. From her sudden widowhood began a new stage in therapy in which Sasha was able to go deeper.

> Craniosacral therapy allowed me to make contact with my pain and experience it deeply, not from victimhood, but from awareness. I discovered the enormous emotional, psychological and physical wear I had been subjecting myself to, trying to change my external circumstances, but without going to the source of my own suffering, my own fears and shortcomings. We then moved on to a verbal exchange therapy. At the beginning, it was very little at first, I was afraid of feeling so vulnerable.

She then began a therapy that the patient herself called a "rebirthing" therapy. It was crucial to discover that she had been disconnected from herself. Once she overcame her panic attacks, it was possible to work through the various overlapping griefs: the loss of her husband; the loss of the family she was unable to build; the loss of her role as a mother; and the loss of her own femininity.

The therapeutic work was mainly focused on enabling Sasha to initiate such mourning processes as were necessary to recover a deeply wounded femininity and a self-esteem that until then had been based on job performance and not on self-confidence or self-assurance.

There were numerous and deep therapeutic conversations in which the patient was able to speak freely.

At the same time, it was important to create an emotional environment that leads to the reunion of the mother with her child. It was time to recover or, rather, to rebuild a healthy relationship between the two. At the beginning it was a very complex process in which both felt lost and had to articulate a family again, without the authoritarian father figure that had separated them. They had to move from dysfunctionality to functionality.

The son did not trust the mother; however, he agreed to come to therapy and a moving process began in which love and tenderness, despite misgivings and fears, made their way like a stream of water that resumes its natural course.

It is important to see how therapy has an almost immediate effect as people recognize their problem and make a mature commitment to overcome it. Sasha and her son continued to come to therapy for a while, and separately. The new level of awareness was the will, which put them in an emotional state of optimism from which it was possible to create change.

She was also able to deepen her rebirth process during a therapeutic trip I organized to India to work on psychological and existential fears, as well as femininity. It was surprising, after so many years of silence, to see her interacting so openly with her travel companions in an atmosphere of joyful and supportive sisterhood.

I was no longer so afraid to show my vulnerability and I didn't mind sharing my experience with other women, even some of my own setting. I talked about what I felt. The moments of intimacy that we experienced as a group were wonderful and very respectful [...] I felt myself blossoming and, from that love for myself that I had discovered, I longed to find love in someone else. I am a person who lives in a couple and in company. Today I feel that I have brought out things in me that were very much hidden and that have allowed me to be more myself and to feel more secure in my current relationship.

A new state of consciousness of acceptance surfaced in Sasha, in which her vision of life was more harmonious and which, through forgiveness, it was possible to achieve transcendence.

The Absent Mother

Ana Maria, a clinical psychologist, seems very self-confident, cheerful and outgoing. She came to therapy seeking help because she could not sleep; she has catastrophic thoughts and a terrible anxiety that oppresses her chest and doesn't let her breathe. Fear is the level of consciousness that prevents her from taking control of her life.

She was referred by a family member to treat a depression caused by her great marital unhappiness after thirty-five years of marriage. In the first sessions of craniosacral therapy, I identified in Ana Maria poor bonding with her mother in her primary age.

This dysfunctional relationship would continue over time and affect the full development of a healthy femininity. The feminine is deeply rooted in the essence of the human being and of life and is present in all genders at the level of the psyche and not exclusively in the genitalia.

It occurs through the maternal bond. If that mother is absent, physically or emotionally, another figure, such as a caregiver, a grandmother, a wet nurse, can repair or reestablish that lost connection. Through skin-to-skin contact, during breastfeeding, or through the most basic maternal expressions of love and tenderness, this condition of femininity develops in human beings, which, beyond gender, will manifest itself in values such as sensitivity, generosity, empathy, intuition and the search for beauty.

Ana Maria studied Psychology at Universidad San Marcos of Lima.

> That's where I met my first husband. A young, charming engineering student. We were married before we graduated. He didn't have a cent. We had a son, and soon after we divorced. Years later I met my second husband, a businessman with an excellent economic position, but he was twenty years older than me. My parents didn't seem to mind that I married such an old man. In fact, my mother only lived to take care of my father. She took little care of the house or of us, her children.

The second husband, in spite of being very attractive and seductive —he dazzled her from the first moment—, turned out to be a sullen, distant and ill-tempered man, and when he found out about Ana Maria's pregnancy, he reacted very badly. He already had children from his first marriage, and its dissolution had been very conflictive. With those children, the relationship was equally bad. He isolated himself in the same house he shared with Ana Maria by setting up a room as if it were a bunker and then totally ignored her. When a second pregnancy came, the reaction was so violent that Ana Maria lost the child. Her level of consciousness according to the Hawkins scale was pain and there Ana Maria could only harbor an enormous dejection, from which it was impossible to find her way out.

> I became pregnant again, but this time he did not dare to assault me. At that time, I wanted to do a master's degree, but I decided not to enroll so that I would not have to interrupt my studies when I gave birth. At that time, I started working.
>
> In the beginning, when the children were small, he was affectionate, although very demanding, and they were terrified of him. I worked hard to support them because he didn't provide anything. He wouldn't let them go to sports tournaments because he said it hurt their school performance. I often took them secretly, because it was very important to them.

The children grew up and Ana Maria wanted to separate, but did not dare. She was anxious about everything and had panic attacks.

In the therapeutic conversations, she became aware of the way her mother had neglected her and resented the lack of love or maternal affection not only for her, but for all her siblings. At this stage of therapy, there were mixed states of shame, guilt and unsatisfied basic desires, which generated emotions that fluctuated between anxiety, humiliation and despair. Also, the fear of feeling and acknowledging these emotions despite being a clinical psychologist and having done psychological work for many years.

On the couch I sensed an anxious person, with quite an altered nervous system. The information emerges from the unconscious practically at the first contact with the therapist's hands: "I am being carried! There is someone who can hold me!"

Maternal abandonment had left deep scars on her psyche, but as we went deeper into therapy, Ana Maria showed signs of regaining her self-confidence.

We began to work on her grief after the separation from a cold husband with whom she had not been able to carry out a life project, and no longer could do so. From then on, she was able to start looking for an apartment to move live apart serenely and without resentment. At first it was a very difficult process, since the children were very worried about their mother's decision, and she, in spite of being resolved, was at a level of consciousness of guilt and from there it was very difficult for her to make assertive decisions to build a new life. However, Ana Maria's performance throughout all those years had been so impeccable, that her children, as a sign of respect and affection, ended up supporting her decision.

Finally, the distancing of Ana Maria and her husband took place with total acceptance, which allowed for forgiveness. Her children, who had managed to recover the relationship with their father, were a great inspiration for her. It is very interesting to see how, through motherhood, she manages to make contact with the feminine and integrate it. Thanks to this, her children, all boys, have assimilated both aspects very well.

After the death of her husband, Ana Maria acknowledges with emotion that, through the eyes of her children, she has been able to discover aspects and qualities of his personality that today make up the paternal legacy that they treasure.

Encouraged by her own success in dealing assertively with a difficult separation in her old age, Ana Maria decided to continue with the COR Method therapy. Today, at seventy-five, she coquettishly confesses that she would like to fall in love again.

The Feminine in Man

We are changing our worldview in many aspects. We see more and more men taking on traditionally feminine roles in terms of childcare and childrearing. In fact, nowadays, in many developed countries, legislation for pre— and postpartum leave for men, who decide to take care of their babies while their mothers work, are being established. This traditional conception of male and female attributions and roles is already considered as outdated. They are past dynamics, which, increasingly, the current generations are abandoning for more egalitarian relationships or, simply, for practicality.

This in terms of roles, but in terms of emotions, men and women with well-integrated feminine and masculine energies can interact in freer ways and thus achieve not only a true connection, but a more complete and harmonious realization as human beings.

In our culture, masculine energy, associated with our ability to think and act, has been used to suppress and control our feminine intuition and sensitivity, rather than to support and express them. But the well-balanced feminine energy in an individual of either sex is a powerful force we can turn to for guidance, power, nurturing and support.

By opening up to his own feminine nature and trusting in it, a man will find in himself all those attributes he has been lacking and the women he relates to will reflect that same energy, being more confident, more authentic and more genuinely loving and compassionate.

The traditional male was taught from an early age to repress the feminine part of himself, which cries out for appreciation and tenderness. It was not uncommon to see this type of men relating to women who were dependent, needy, or who only knew how to express their power through manipulation, frivolity, victimhood or dishonesty.

Rodrigo is an attractive and successful man in his fifties. He decided to come to therapy at the insistence of his wife, who was my patient. The couple was having problems that were threatening their coexistence, but, nevertheless, affection and the desire of both of them to be parents prevailed. When he arrived at my office, I was struck by the sight of a defiant-looking man, dressed like a rebellious teenager. He was quite fed up with being forced to go to therapy, which, according to him, was useless. The handwriting on his chart was childish and messy. That first therapeutic conversation did not yield much information. According to the Hawkins scale, Rodrigo's level of consciousness was that of profound apathy, which made him give up the possibility of changing his life, without even trying. Such was his sense of hopelessness.

The opening took place in the second session. That day he came in a suit and tie and with a more mature and formal attitude. It was as if two clearly antagonistic personalities coexisted in Rodrigo. That day he told me how his family had suffered a misfortune when his younger brother had died after hitting his head hard when he fell from a tree. He vaguely remembered the events, except for that feeling of emotional abandonment of a child who did not understand what was happening around him. Rodrigo angrily recalled how his parents left him at his maternal grandparents' house while they were at the hospital and, after a week, buried his brother, whose life could not be saved. Then came the breakdown of the family life and the inability to handle grief together. Faced with the tragedy of the dead son, the father left their home and the mother, obsessed by her loss, decided to give Rodrigo to his grandparents, with whom he ended up growing up. Rodrigo's relationship with his mother became distant. She, unable to recover from the tragedy and her husband's abandonment, decided to work without respite. Rodrigo spoke of her as a strong person, with mettle, a tireless worker; values that he looked for in a woman as a partner, rather than other more feminine attributes, such as tenderness, companionship, emotional connection.

> I really received love from my grandparents. They were the two exceptional people in my life who made me feel loved for the first time. My grandfather, in fact, died in my arms of a heart attack. That second event had a huge emotional impact on my life.

A tragic vision of life manifested itself in a permanent state of suffering and discouragement in Rodrigo's life, from where it was impossible to create the energy needed to initiate the healing of the soul.

With Gestalt therapy we were able to manage his immense anger at the feeling of abandonment that had been with him since he was a child. In one session, he even crawled around looking for his mother. There were still many unresolved issues in his life, many unfinished situations that needed to be restructured so that he could integrate them and move on. The tragic death of his only sibling, the abandonment by his mother and the death of his maternal grandfather were registered in the child as traumatic events. However, rage is a state of consciousness superior to suffering. Rage functions in this case as fuel for the individual to get out of states of despondency and discouragement, from which therapeutic work becomes very difficult.

It was an arduous, intense process, but Rodrigo finally managed to assume his responsibility as an adult man in his personal life. From then on, another phase of therapy began, with greater sensitivity, maturity and commitment.

With Gestalt therapy many of Rodrigo's emotional and bonding problems could emerge into consciousness, but there was still a lot of pain energetically embedded in his body. Rodrigo had severe headaches, high blood pressure, irrational fears. So, in the following sessions I introduced craniosacral therapy to work from another level: body awareness.

> It took almost three years working on my relationship with my mother so I was able to "forgive" her for what I felt had been abandonment. I had a lot of anger. I asked my mother to come to therapy with me one day and that session was very liberating for both of us.

For Rodrigo it was very important to work on the relationship with the mother, who did not have a well-integrated maternal-feminine aspect. This great emptiness of his masculinity in search of the feminine was permanently manifested in very precarious relationships and always from the affective dependence of the abandoned child who was looking for the partner to satisfy all his emotional deficiencies.

From a new awareness, Rodrigo was able to understand the origin of his problems in his relationships with women. In fact, his love life began with a failed love affair.

> I remember the betrayal of my first partner, to whom I gave myself unreservedly, very much in love. This left a mark of great pain, to such an extent that I have always feared and expected infidelity in all my subsequent relationships.

After several sessions, Rodrigo recognized that he had become a jealous man, unable to handle his insecurity, unable to express his emotions and communicate his innermost feelings.

Thanks to the closure of unprocessed grief, Rodrigo was able to recover his relationship with his mother, reconnect with her and with that feminine aspect in him. All this was necessary to allow him to show his vulnerable aspects and his great sensitivity. Paradoxically, the fact that he sought out women with a very strong character — like his maternal model — made his insecurity more acute, which led him to react with macho responses to protect himself.

> Although I went to therapy to please my wife, this meant a real discovery of deep aspects of my personality, unsuspected even by myself.

A new state of consciousness was opening up at this stage, that of neutrality or the capacity to perceive facts without a burden of judgment, without a negative label. This undoubtedly made him gain confidence in himself and in life. This represented, to a large extent, a liberation from his permanent state of suffering.

Craniosacral therapy was fundamental for Rodrigo to reconnect with his own soul and allowed him to release a lot of repressed pain. It was a period of transcendence and growth, also within his relationship.

> We managed to reach a period of greater stability; we began to do projects together; we had the long-awaited child. I supported my wife a lot so that she could also become a professional. I helped her with the investment to set up her ophthalmology clinic. She was very happy at that time, we got along very well. It was a nice period of the relationship, although my fear of infidelity and abandonment was always latent.

Suddenly, everything started to become very intense for Rodrigo and again he did not know how to express his emotions, nor understand what was happening to him. He relapsed into alcohol and this provoked explosions and often violent reactions.

> By then, I felt misunderstood by my wife and began to detach emotionally.

Rodrigo resented his wife because she did not accept him as he was. It did not take long for this feeling of rejection to make him seek attention and affection in an extramarital relationship, which made things much more complicated for both of them. This prevailing tendency to feel abandoned caused Rodrigo to return again to therapy seeking to recover the adult Rodrigo. The level of excision of the trauma has a lot to do with the patient's ability to overcome a traumatic event.

The couple could not overcome the constant mutual reproaches, nor find a meeting point to continue their life together. She, who had also suffered abandonment as a child when she lost her mother to cancer, childishly demanded that Rodrigo fill her emotional void. The relationship became very conflicted. They finally decided to separate. However, Rodrigo continues to care for his three children with touching dedication and devotion. The eldest son, the product of a previous relationship with his wife, whom Rodrigo took as his own when he was only a few months old, and the twins they had, continue to be an important link with his ex-wife. They have managed to maintain a civilized and respectful relationship for the sake of raising their children. Both are now more mature and, in his case, Rodrigo has been able to regain his self-confidence, which today allows him to be a man who is not afraid to show his feelings and express them with complete honesty.

Chapter 7
Why Me? When Tragedy Bursts into Our Lives

The concept of tragedy, in its strict meaning that comes from the Greeks, is that dramatic work in which characters of great value, known as heroes, are driven to a terrible and irremediable end. For the purpose of this reflection, we are interested in saving the objective of this dramatic genre: to create a purifying effect in the spectator and, in our case, in the people who suffer a tragic event in their own flesh. Tragedy, for what it carries in itself, no longer as a mere moral teaching, is a promise of redemption through asking ourselves who we really are and why we have come to this world.

Friedrich Nietzsche[17] said that *"tragedy does not instill resignation or denial of life, nor the inevitability of suffering, but affirms life itself in all its afflictions"*.

Tragedy bursts into the lives of human beings, who, limited in their power of decision and action in the face of it, helplessly contemplate the brutal interruption of the existing order in their lives. The daily disposition of existence is shattered and the course of the individual's destiny is decisively affected. This translates into suffering, which is consubstantial to the human experience.

Tragedy, misfortune or "the bad hour", represents only a moment, a single second is enough to know it, and many times a lifetime to learn to live with its aftermath of uncertainty and desolation. Tragedy isolates us from everything and from ourselves. It leaves us unable to respond, unprotected in the face of a reality that seems unjust and undeserved. And yet, when we think that we will not be able to bear it, that we will die or lose our minds, the strength of the soul or the instinct of survival comes to our rescue and we cling to life.

Tragedy, therefore, relates us to our own fragility, confronts us with reality and with what we don't know about ourselves, but which will determine who we will be. With tragedy there is no escape: indifference and non-acceptance vanish. Madness may be a response, but it is an unhealthy response.

Unlike the classical Greek tragedy of Aeschylus, in which the hero knows he is the instrument of the wishes of the gods and cannot fail to fulfill his destiny, tragedy for modern man, using Shakespeare's characters as an example, involves anguish before the consequences of his own actions, before the doubt of having been able to do one thing or the other; the guilt for not having been or for not having listened to that warning in time and, in short, the agony of facing himself and his destiny.

However, although tragedy can be considered the cause of many misfortunes, it also holds the mystery and the possibility of penetrating into the profound truth of things.

The greater the misfortune of the Greek heroes, the more exalted was the hymn to their courage and glory. This, undoubtedly, is the most important lesson left by the ancients to posterity: a human greatness that is drawn not only from the exploits of a warrior, but also from his spiritual strength in the midst of fatality.

It is not in vain, the end of great dramatic works throughout history makes us sympathize with the misfortune of the main character, but at the same time we are filled with hope and inspiration when we see how he is reborn in a dimension that transcends any suffering of the flesh and produces the triumph of the spirit.

The Pain That Awakens Us

The COR Method shows us how in the very suffering of tragedy, we can find the paths to reach the awakening of consciousness and to live a powerful transformation as human beings. If we manage to overcome resentment, the need for revenge, bitterness over injustice or the non-acceptance of an inexorable reality that overcomes us and leaves us immobilized, we will be on the threshold of a life with new meanings and purpose.

In tragedy we need to rely on empathic listening, because pain needs another human being to validate it, to legitimize it in order for it to dissolve. Pain needs witnesses in order to be repaired. The person who has suffered a tragedy needs to verbalize and the COR Method provides the space, respect, time and presence for this. It is important to let the person see the resources that are emerging to help them process what they are experiencing; to re-touch the most painful images to restructure their meanings and observe how life is projected after what happened.

Accompanying my patients in times of crisis and painful experiences has been a constant source of learning for me. Relieving them and helping them overcome their tragedies has served me as invaluable training in compassion and empathy; but seeing them grow spiritually and learn to live fully, despite their great losses, without a doubt, is what inspires me and gives meaning to my work. The COR Method seeks that the individual is able to get in touch with his or her pain and go through the phases of grief without clinging to a life of suffering. For this reason, I consider it of great importance and help, to share with those who read this book the following testimonies of life and redemption, which I quote below with deep respect and admiration.

Oriana and the Perfect Life

Oriana was thirty-one when she experienced the tragic event that changed her life and that of her entire family. We did a very in-depth job, in which I was able to accompany her to process her enormous loss in all the phases of her grief. An arduous task that was possible thanks to Oriana's intelligence and resilience.

Her testimony expresses in such a sensitive, human and authentic way the process she went through, from the very moment of the accident, and during the whole time she was taking care of her son, as well as the change of consciousness she experienced, to which I have decided not to add any further comments from my perspective as a therapist.

> I lived in fear. My best friend didn't understand why I was afraid: with a model husband who was doing well in business; the children I had always dreamed of, two girls and two boys; well off; fulfilled as a designer; fulfilled as a mother. And that was exactly what I was afraid of: the perfection of my life. I saw that everything came easy to me; I wanted something and I got it, sometimes without making the slightest effort. Every night I prayed and asked God to take away that fear because I was aware that I had not made the slightest effort to have everything I had, but I did not want to lose it.
>
> We were all at home and I went out to buy some flowers; my husband stayed with the children. At a moment when the nanny who was taking care of the little one, my fourth child, my one-and-a-half-year-old baby, went to the bathroom and left him

alone in the garden, the baby drowned in the pool. My husband pulled him out of the water. I arrived home right away because I was called, and found that tragedy. He became a complete vegetable: a quadriplegic with cerebral palsy, and he stayed that way for six years until he died.

Claudia was recommended to me by a friend three days after the accident. She told me that she had been thinking a lot about the best way to help me and asked me to authorize her to bring Claudia to the clinic for craniosacral therapy for the baby. In those first days, the child was very stressed because it was just when the sedation had been removed and a channel had been opened for him to breathe. Claudia started touching him and I remember hearing the child make a sigh of relief. After that visit he was able to sleep soundly and peacefully.

After Claudia saw my son, I asked her to take care of me too because I didn't know how to handle the whole situation. I was drowning, but I couldn't cry because my husband was completely collapsed. I remember the first time I went to therapy with Claudia. I lay down on the couch, closed my eyes and cried and cried for about an hour; then I fell deeply asleep, and in the dream, I saw my son playing with some pebbles in a spring. It was the first time after the accident that I dreamed about my son. After that, I continued with Claudia. Going to her office was like unplugging me from all the information I was handling inside my head; plus caring for my other three children; plus my husband, who was in a terrible depression that we could not get him out of; plus my parents, looking down on me with a great sadness that was breaking my soul; plus all the problems around me to solve. I felt that if I turned off my engine, everything would shut down.

I think I was still in shock and on autopilot, writing my *to-do list*. I never felt pain. I didn't allow myself to cry. I was not in touch with my emotional side. I wanted to be practical and resolute. I had no time or the chance to fall apart. I was like iron, like an impenetrable log. I remember that I felt very strong, I would not allow anyone to come and talk to me about sad things, or to feel sorry for me. I was always on the defensive.

This therapy was like my recharge. I came twice or even three times a week. At first, Claudia did craniosacral therapy for me. I only received bad news from the doctors, so I unloaded a lot with her. A very strange energy surrounded me: there was the child, but there was also my husband, who didn't want to get out of bed; and one of my daughters, who was also depressed and having problems at school. She was rebellious and talkative and was being kicked out of the classroom. The other girl was alone all the time and didn't want to leave her room. I knew they were suffering, but I didn't have time to take care of them. The younger brother was glued to his little brother all day and treated him as if nothing had happened to him and slept with him. And me, trying to solve all the problems and worrying that my children would not be bullied at school.

I Feel Blessed

I never imagined that I could say that I was being blessed with what happened to me... It is very difficult to understand. It's not that I feel that it had to happen to me so I could learn what I have learned, but now I am full of gratitude and I see life in a very different way. Despite the tragedy and all the problems, I felt very privileged because everything I set out to do to help my son, I was able to do; all the necessary resources were there. I could count on the best doctors and therapists, the number one in all areas; we had access to the most advanced treatments, etc. I gave my son Andres everything I never thought I could give him in my life.

Never in six and a half years was I alone with him for more than ten minutes. I was always accompanied and everyone who came in contact with the child fell in love with him. All the people around him were good people, they never failed me, not a nurse, not a therapist, no one.

I think the communication between him and me went beyond just seeing each other. Yes, I touched him and kissed him a lot, but I felt that we were communicating on another plane. I knew when he was feeling bad; I knew when something was making him uncomfortable. It was a strange connection. Of course, he couldn't tell me anything, but I felt it. One time I had some very bad pains in my abdomen. I contacted the best ultrasound professional in the country and asked him to do an abdominal echo on my son because I was sure he had something, because I felt a lot of pain in my stomach and for me that was our way of communicating. The echoes were done and, indeed, he had eighteen stones in his bladder. I arranged to have him operated on in the United States. In the meantime, I told this to Claudia, who, by the way, saw my son four hours a week and never charged a penny for it. She was the only one who could bring peace to the boy. When she saw him, he relaxed and slept pleasantly, which was practically impossible to achieve, even with medication. When Claudia put him to sleep, he looked like a healthy child, showing no signs of the problem that afflicted him. She did not agree to operate on him and told me she wanted to work on him energetically. When we arrived in the United States, all the tests were repeated. Of the eighteen stones, not a single one remained. We returned to Caracas that same day. With Andres we experienced many incidents of this type.

So, why do I say that I felt blessed? Because I saw the miracles; I saw all the opportunities; I saw all the open roads. When I was at Duke Hospital and I walked the halls, I saw babies and children alone, cared for by the hospital staff because their parents had to work. I saw terrible things: children with deformities and diseases and syndromes. Seeing everything I saw in the hospital, the suffering of others, helped me not to feel that my case was the worst, and to be grateful that, in the midst of it all, we had been blessed. There were parents who did not have the means to pay for their children's therapies and some even abandoned them.

Claudia's Therapy

I went through all phases of her therapy. It depended on the state I was in. She did craniosacral therapy, therapeutic conversation, Gestalt therapy, meditation... Although I didn't do well with meditation because of my attention deficit. At first, there wasn't much she could do with me because I was like a log. We were able to go deeper over time. I'm eleven years into it now. It's all very subtle. I felt like I was an onion that was having layers peeled off. I don't remember much of what happened in therapy. Many times, I fell into a very deep sleep. I only know that, when I woke up, I felt more energetic and it was easier for me to perceive things; it was easier for me to tolerate them. Many times, I did not understand why I could not feel sad, but grateful to see all the blessings that surrounded me: for starters, my family. We ended up closer than ever.

Claudia had discharged me four days before Andres' passing, so I immediately contacted her again. She had already told me that I was ready to face and handle all the challenges that would continue to appear in my life. She told me that she would always be there, but that I didn't need to go every week, that I no longer needed "the crutches". I remember crying so hard. I felt like I was being abandoned! Now I continue going to Claudia, but in a spaced manner.

I no longer come to cry, nor to unload, nor do I come to unplug. I feel that there are things I still need to understand. I would like to be more attentive, less scattered, less distracted. I would like to manage my emotions and feelings better. Sometimes I am very explosive and I don't like that part of me. I need to work on me. This is more personal and goes beyond a one-time crisis. I knew the ultimate expression of grief, which is losing a child. I'm not saying that it doesn't hurt anymore, but I have learned to live with it and move on. In spite of everything, I feel that I can help others, people who are going through similar situations to the ones I went through. I would like to be more efficient so I can help more people, in a more practical and less emotional way, without getting so involved.

I knew he had to go, but I always asked God to take him when we were all calm, at peace, so that I could accept it. If Andres had left immediately after the accident, I have no doubt that my husband would have committed suicide and I would have lost my husband as well. I feel that would have ended the lives of my other children. I don't think they would have been able to overcome the tragedy and go on with their lives normally. The time he was with us was the time we needed to prepare ourselves.

I always liked to be surrounded by people, to be among lots of people; all the meetings were held at my house, but after this happened to me, I can't stand crowds anymore. I can't stand the crowds, the noise, it bothers me. There are many things I have not been able to overcome yet.

I have always been a perfectionist and Andrés taught me that life is not perfect. I was too intense and demanding with my children and, in my determination to make them perfect, I stopped enjoying things about each of the older ones because of the stress in which I lived. Andres came to show me the immaturity that was hiding behind my perfectionism.

I feel the need to give, for all that I have received. Giving knowledge, information, acknowledgements, doing good deeds. I feel that I owe so much and I have the feeling that I never give enough, if I think of all that I have received.

Lorenzo: from "Why Me" to Unlimited Awareness

I'm Lorenzo, I'm thirty-six, and I suffered an accident three years ago. I was shot and paralyzed from my chest to my feet. The bullet caused a spinal cord injury that prevented me from walking again. Today I'm in a wheelchair.

Researching the best medical options for my case, I decided to come with my partner to the United States hoping to improve my situation, but also to have access to a life as normal as possible. It has not been easy. This is much more expensive, but here we are, fighting every day. The accident was in 2015. In 2016 I got married, and in 2017 Mario, our son, was born. In our search, we came across an excellent physiotherapist. In her office there was a person who did craniosacral therapy and my wife became very interested in the subject. Then we began to investigate who was doing this therapy in Venezuela and that is how we came to Claudia, who, we learned later, had been a student of John Upledger, the creator of SCT. My wife, Maria Elena, went first for a chronic cervical ailment she'd had for fifteen years or more. After several sessions, she was very insistent that I see Claudia, so I made an appointment.

Lorenzo came to my practice through his partner, who was my patient. He constantly brought me his experience, since his conscience was very connected to his consciousness. He came with a lot of pain, despite having worked a lot on the physical level. I sensed from the first moment that Lorenzo was unconsciously looking for more psychological support. He had learned to be independent despite the paraplegia. In fact, I remember the agile way he climbed onto the craniosacral therapy couch, without any help, thanks to the strength he had developed in his arms.

> The experience was indescribable. The craniosacral therapy that I had undergone in the United States was very good, but Claudia takes it to another level, because she complements it with other types of therapies and the treatment is much more comprehensive, and this gave me a lot of confidence. The place where she does the therapy is more than just an office, it is a place with a very powerful energy and you feel better just by entering.

Lorenzo had decided to learn to live with his new reality as best he could, even though he still harbored some hope of regaining mobility. It was admirable to see his ability to adapt to a limited physical condition, but one that he took on without any victimhood.

> After the accident, my family was very insistent that I see a psychologist and one came to see me several times at home, but I was fine, at least I thought I was. People were surprised that I had

not fallen into depression. Of course, I had trouble adjusting to this new situation, but I think I coped reasonably well.

The craniosacral therapy here at the medical center I attend in Florida is manual only and I must say it is very good, but it lacks that psychological and spiritual aspect that Claudia brings to her treatment. I felt great empathy for her and that feeling of being understood even without having to explain myself. Little by little, information that I didn't even know about myself emerged and has encouraged me to continue exploring and deepening my self-knowledge.

With Gestalt therapy, Lorenzo was able to establish real contact with the trauma he had experienced and with his sense of loss, and he became fully aware of what he had in his life before and after the accident.

I was able to go much deeper and understand that I had been hiding my emotions throughout the whole period following the accident that led to my paralysis. I discovered myself as a person with a tendency to repress my emotions. Thanks to this therapy, I was able to make contact with what I was really feeling. At that moment I really began to mourn what I had lost.

It would seem that Lorenzo had accepted his circumstance, but in the first sessions, I could see that he was unconsciously harboring expectations of healing.

I admit that when I first went to Claudia, I expected to start regaining mobility. That was my hope and also my goal. When she gave me the first sessions and included the psychological part and meditation, I began to discover more important aspects inside me than just being able to move my legs. This is very difficult to explain, but I felt like an inner spark that awakened other things in me that I had not discovered, that I did not know existed. She helped me understand that thanks to that spark I had not fallen into depression, but now I was aware of it. My limitation, until that moment, was not only physical, but spiritual as well.

Lorenzo, despite his new condition, is a man with impressive vital energy. He has always been the mainstay of his home and a great pillar for his wife, who faced difficult times as a result of emigrating and later with the pregnancy and the care of their baby.

Life doesn't stop and we are in a permanent learning process. This last year has been quite challenging because we had a child and no help. Fourteen months of little sleep, of taking care of the baby, of working, of keeping the house. We also emigrated, changed countries, everything has been like a tornado!

I feel that I matured in this period. But not only because of the accident itself. Without the therapy it is very possible that I would have remained in a state of victim consciousness, wondering: why me, why can't I walk again? But I became aware of many things. It was like discovering another Lorenzo. Many people don't know who they are completely until a drastic change comes upon them. Despite the wheelchair, this new awakening self was free.

When I look at my life in retrospect, I become aware of the transformation I have undergone and am still going through. One day I got shot and the next day I am a paraplegic. I lived the previous thirty-three years in one way: playing soccer, going to the gym, and now my body is different. My vision of life has changed profoundly. I cared about other things; but, above all, I cared about my physical appearance, dressing well, looking good.

Of course, I still take care of my body and my health, but now I am more focused on my wife and my son. I care about them and their happiness and about continuing to grow as a human being.

Right now, I am very excited because I have discovered in myself the ability to inspire others and I would like to develop some coaching skills and some public speaking skills, to help other people. That possibility gives great meaning to my life. In the same way, I believe that physically I can continue to improve. I continue with my regular therapies and with Claudia. With the check-scan technique, in some sessions, I have been able to feel larger parts of my legs and even in the abdomen area.

Professionally, I would like to get more involved in technology and digital features. I plan, now that I am in the United States, to set up a cryptocurrency company and everything that is trading between them, to exchange and to be able to offer an investment service in digital currencies to customers. I want to develop that project and continue with the family business in Venezuela. I want to get back to exercising. Before I had our son, I exercised permanently as part of my therapy, but now I have slowed down.

This is not a concluded therapy; there were crucial moments of Lorenzo's awakening and important advances, but there is still a lot of work ahead. The physical distance between therapist and patient has not been an insurmountable obstacle, but Lorenzo's day-to-day dynamics mean that we have to adapt the therapy to his pace and possibilities.

Today, I live at a much deeper dimension, asking myself what we have come here for. Far from continuing to see what happened to me as a tragedy, I now have the certainty that everything that happens to us in life is an opportunity for expansion, growth and evolution.

Sonia and the Rebirth

I was born on July 4, 1978. In Caracas. Vaginal delivery, full term. Overweight at birth.

In this way, which leaves no doubt about it, we are introduced to Sonia, a young doctor, who from a very young age was clear about her vocation.

I remember when my younger sister was born. I was eight years old. She was born with a skull fracture. She had to have emergency surgery. It was my first experience with disease and it had a strong impact on me. My parents took her abroad. They were away for a month. When they came back with my sister healthy, I told them I wanted to be a doctor. The doctors saved my sister and thus my family. I wanted to save others as well.

For Sonia, medicine was everything, her career was her great passion. However, she tells us how in the fourth year of her studies, when she began to learn forensic medicine and had to go to the morgue, she experienced a very traumatic shock.

It was very different seeing sick patients from seeing corpses. I hadn't had such close contact with death until then. Besides, there was a very dark energy in the morgue. There I saw that ugly face of the human being: crime. It was Dantesque.

I got married, had two children, and stopped practicing medicine to devote myself to them. I went to therapy for the first time in my life because my eldest child had problems and was reluctant to learn to swim. My pregnancy with her was difficult; my father was dying and I was the one taking care of him. The child psychologist recommended that I seek professional help for myself. This is how I met Claudia. In therapy, many things came to the surface that I had taken for granted in my life, but that were still latent and causing suffering. I associated their origin with very difficult situations that I lived through, such as the death of my father, then my mother's illness and the heart surgery that my young son underwent.

Craniosacral therapy is an excellent technique to detect and bring to the surface traumatic situations that the psyche has tried to "encapsulate" due to the inability to manage the experience, which produces a kind of "energy cyst" in the body, just as the physical body when it receives an aggression creates a hematoma to protect the rest of the body tissue.

Although Sonia decided to go to therapy for a very specific reason —helping her daughter with her panic over water—, when she lay down on the couch, she did not really know what she would come into contact with; what memories or emotions would emerge during therapy.

Her trust in me as a therapist and a strong commitment to her personal growth process allowed her to go very deep; to touch her vulnerability and all the transformative potential that was waiting to be awakened.

> From the first time I put myself in her hands, I felt very protected and supported. Every time I lay down on the couch for craniosacral therapy, I felt how Claudia, without barely touching me, carried me and that gave me a feeling of tranquility and peace.
>
> Since I was feeling well and in balance, I had stopped going to therapy for a while, but the situation of political instability in the country was increasing. My husband, who noticed I was

anxious, suggested I return to therapy. A family member and another person very close to us had been imprisoned. The street was very hot and the political climate was heated, and I was certainly extremely anxious. There was a very tense atmosphere in my house.

The night before the tragedy, I went to my therapy session with Claudia. I couldn't stop crying and I didn't know why. I was immensely anxious that night. Now I think it was a premonition. The next day I went with the children to a fair at school and when I came back, my husband had decided to go biking with a good friend of his. I was waiting for him at home with my two children, but the hours passed and I had no news of him. At five o'clock in the afternoon, I received a call and was told that there had been a situation with my husband. Immediately, I thought that he had fallen down a ravine and that maybe he had fractured or hit his head and they were taking him to the hospital. As the hours went by, I was told that he had been kidnapped. I remember perfectly well every minute and every moment, every conversation and everything that happened that afternoon. The two families got together and started talking about paying ransom. I remember that I wrote to Claudia to tell her what was happening. Those were hours of great anxiety and I was beginning to feel that something very bad had happened. By nightfall, I had a very strong feeling that my husband was dead. The next day, we were informed that he and his friend had been killed. I was already dressed all in black because I could feel it.

When I heard what had happened, I immediately went to Sonia's house. I found her lying on the lawn in the garden, tearing her hair and clothes, drooling and looking lost. I took her by the shoulders and repeatedly asked her to look me in the eye; I asked for carrots to be brought to force her to bite and swallow. It was important to keep Sonia from suffering a psychotic episode and the only way to avoid this was to bring her back to the present and confront her with what was happening, no matter how strong it was.

> Then I understood what it was to go crazy, because at times I was afraid I was losing my mind... My body and my mind simply could not handle that information. And it was very scary because it was like leaving my body. I vaguely remember when Claudia arrived. She looked me in the eyes and asked me to fix my gaze. I tried, but I couldn't, I didn't want to... I avoided looking at her for fear of seeing what was happening and knowing that everything had really happened. The memory of that day is horrible. I couldn't talk about it without crying. It is very painful and it is a scar that will never fade. It was heartbreaking, a lot of confusion, a lot of denial. I needed to look for someone to blame, to find reasons. I was in a very serious state of shock and denial.

Tragedy will always leave traces. The emotions that emerge as a result of it will tell us much of what we do not know about ourselves; it will leave incisions in our psyche and with them we will have to continue our lives, because unlike what is believed, there is no before and after: life is a process; a continuum through which we all transform ourselves. The COR Method involves a therapeutic preparation so that the patient can accept the inevitable; to accept death, illness, losses; in short, to accept and assume change; to overcome trauma, denial and through pain achieve a true transformation of our consciousness.

It was a very hard period. My son's illness, my father's illness, my mother's illness and then the death of my husband. Between the ages of thirty and thirty-five I experienced the most drastic changes in my life.

When my husband died, I was devastated. I had such intense pain in my chest. It was hard to think. But I wanted to look for options to mitigate the pain other than anxiolytics or antidepressants. I didn't want to suppress my emotions.

Sonia was afraid of getting sick and had many reservations about traditional medication, because her mother relied almost exclusively on pharmaceuticals.

My mother has Parkinson's, cognitive disorders and psychosis. She became ill with lung cancer after dad's death. It was all very abrupt. Mom literally went crazy. She could not stand the pain. With Claudia I did craniosacral therapy, meditations, and all this combined helped me a lot in my grieving process. Over time, as I progressed in my therapy, I felt Luis, my husband, in a different way: not with pain, but with gratitude for what we had experienced. In many of the craniosacral therapy sessions, I was able to relive our life as a couple, our experiences, our travels, our love, the way I made many things about him, his personality, my own.

So, at the age of thirty-five I found myself widowed, with a five-year-old daughter and a three-year-old son with a heart condition that required special treatments. At that time, I decided to emigrate and return to work. It was clear that I would not be able to practice my profession as a doctor abroad and that I would have to start from scratch. I began to evaluate my options and the only thing that was clear to me was that my passion had always been to take care of patients. It was then that I began to study Oriental medicine. Undoubtedly, the confidence I gained from the craniosacral therapy I received from Claudia and the positive results it had produced in me were very important in the paradigm shift I experienced from my vision of allopathic medicine to traditional oriental medicine.

I tell people who are going through a critical situation, "You're not going to die from this. You're going to get through it." Because in those moments, what you really feel is that you can't take the pain anymore. And you have to keep living one day at a time. The pain is so great that I felt like an elephant was crushing my chest and would not let me breathe. I had anxiety crises, panic crises, I could cry for hours without stopping. The pain was paralyzing. If it hadn't been for my two children, I don't know what would have become of me, because they were the great reasons for me to go on and find another meaning to my life. I saw them and I knew that I could not allow myself to die. And that is why I had my reservations about the medication. I kept telling myself: "I have to be healthy; I have to be conscious; I have to be well and I have to get up every day and prepare breakfast". Going to another therapy different from Claudia's would have been perhaps more similar to what my family did and that unfortunately did not bring good results for them. Today I feel that there has been an awakening in me and in all the people around me.

Now I look back and wonder how I was able to move forward, after so much pain and feeling so disoriented. I had lost my partner, my country, my status, because I was now a widow and an immigrant, with my family scattered, and a career that was now of no use to me. The ground had been moved. All I had was myself and my two children.

I continued to accompany Sonia therapeutically when she moved to the United States. At first, she even had to overcome her fear of applying for a student visa. The therapies were done via Skype and, the first time I had to travel to the US, I visited her in her new home. It was very satisfying to see how she progressed and how she gave incredibly creative answers to all the challenges that came her way.

Today I am full of gratitude and I would like my experience to be useful to other people. I would also like to encourage people to be open to new therapies. In fact, I did my thesis on health practices through alternative means. I went to a therapeutic group for widows and that also helped me. Unfortunately, though, the percentage of people who are open to these kinds of alternative therapies is very low.

When I began to study traditional Chinese medicine, I raised my hand every five minutes to question everything they said. I came from studying for ten years in my country, from being a medical surgeon, and that still conditioned me a lot. But there was something that had a positive impact on me. One day I had to miss a class in the morning and go to another one in the evening to make it up. The teacher did not know me. In the middle of the class, he turned to me and asked:

"Are you mourning?"

"How do you know?" I asked.

"Are you aware that you can't stop coughing?"

"Yes, but what does that have to do with it?"

"The lung is connected to sadness and that cough reflects a very deep sadness and pain that you are trying to suppress."

I thought, the teacher was not a doctor, but a witch doctor! I began to understand how everything was connected. He put me through a very strong treatment, which at first made me cough a lot, but then I stopped coughing for good.

I was learning how every organ is connected to an emotion, how emotions can make you sick.

I used to see patients for a diagnosis, but now I see them in a more complete way. It is a different way of questioning, of connecting with the patient. Today a blood test and an X-ray are not enough to evaluate a patient. I need to talk to them, see their look, their energy, the emotion they are feeling. That tells me much more.

I try to prescribe medicines that are natural. But I know when it is necessary to prescribe an antibiotic. They go hand in hand.

Emotional aspects are taken into account much more in eastern medicine than in western medicine. We pay the western doctor when we are sick, but we pay the eastern doctor when we are healthy and stop paying when we get sick. I am fascinated by this now! I think the world is becoming more aware and moving towards healthier living.

Right now, my goal is to start working. It has been a very strong personal challenge for me to emigrate with two children. I have just turned forty and I have not ceased to study. I would like all my effort to have meaning and, of course, a financial reward that will allow me to support my children and myself.

These testimonies can leave us speechless. And many will even ask themselves: how can so much suffering be tolerated? We assume that it is natural for children to bury their parents and not the other way around. On the other hand, how can we explain to ourselves that violence can in a single instant condemn a young man to live as a paraplegic in a wheelchair or a family to be left without a father and husband?

Life as we know it is full of tragic events and, although at times it may seem very difficult to overcome, human nature has the potential energy and psychological resource to overcome all kinds of losses. Tragedy comes to touch our souls and, in some way, to change the course of our lives, but never from a position of victimhood. It is a crucial moment that forces us to get in touch with our own essence and to extract from the painful experience the "whys and wherefores" that will lead us to find the true meaning of our existence.

Chapter 8
Self-esteem and Loss: the Persistence of Life

In recent years, and as a product of my own experience in my personal process, I have focused mainly on helping to strengthen people's self-esteem. For this, it has been crucial to understand how to process the mourning of what we lose during our lives.

Each individual and each society has its own ways of processing grief. What is common is that we all need the courage to acknowledge the loss. Many people come to therapy without a clear understanding of why they came. In general, I observe the amount of grief that many of these people have gone through without being able to process it.

We can recognize that we have lost old ways of living, of relating, of mobilizing, of consuming. Of course, not all of us deal with them in the same way. The elaboration of grief is a very personal process of growth that will depend to a great extent on the self-esteem of each one of us. It is important to be aware that every day something is being born and dying; every day we are conquering and losing something.

A good and solid self-esteem favors or ensures an appropriate elaboration of grief. However, the inability to work through a loss leads to existential suffering, often in a chronic manner.

As we have said, one of the fundamental goals of the COR Method is to help the patient to reach the necessary courage to begin the process of overcoming his or her loss. From there we will be able to get in touch with our loss and we will be able to process it and elaborate the grief. Below that level we will feel like victims of everything that happens to us.

Throughout the life cycle, it is inevitable that situations of pain will occur because of what we have lost or left behind. Life confronts us with the possibility of losing something that was important to us: a loved one, the country we left, a relationship, a job, our health. In some cases, the amputation of a limb, the loss of one of the senses, or bodily functions. Experiencing grief is one of the most important psychological processes from a therapeutic point of view —no matter what technique is used to work on it—, because it allows the individual to recover from his or her losses and integrate them as necessary and inevitable life experiences.

Life, although challenging, deserves to be lived, because it is wonderful, but we can only reach that conclusion when self-esteem is solid.

Grief work is of vital importance and of varying length over time. This process may be more intuitive for some and much more challenging for others. Resistance to accepting the loss is rigidity: it is death. On the contrary, acceptance without resistance is persistence: it is life.

Thanks to the grieving process, the psyche can self-repair after a loss. Recovery or preservation of self-esteem is possible. Losses usually cause damage or a decrease in our self-esteem. Losing a job, for example, can affect the way we value ourselves. I may think that I was fired because I was not well qualified, or I may think that the layoff occurred for company budgetary reasons. We can only recover our passion and enthusiasm if we understand that our self-esteem depends on who we are, how we see life, and how we behave with ourselves and others; if we understand that our worth does not depend on what we have lost. A person with high self-esteem can assign meaning to the loss and work through the grief. Similarly, they develop strength when they have been able to overcome other past grief. A person with low self-esteem will tend to fall into pathological grief.

Many people confess to me that they find it difficult to understand what my "evolution and change therapy" means. I have always been fully aware that we are constantly evolving and changing. Processing these transformations is what allows us to move forward. If we do not accept life's changes, we stagnate. From that state, it is not possible to evolve as human beings. The greater our self-esteem, the greater our courage to see ourselves and embark on the path of self-knowledge and healing.

There are multiple intelligences, but evolutionary intelligence refers to the capacity we have to learn while we are learning. Evolution is given by the way in which the species connects with the outside world and responds to its stimuli.

Self-esteem is the awareness and appreciation of your own life; it is knowing how to recognize that you can create and sustain life, that you can evolve. Self-esteem is respect for oneself; it is having personal integrity, the responsibility to assume oneself as one is; to assert oneself. If there is self-esteem, there is purpose.

Many of the problems that people bring to consultation have their origin in low, or bruised self-esteem.

Self-esteem is based on two fundamental factors:

- the individual's sense of security that he or she has all the necessary resources to cope with difficulties;
- the feeling that we deserve to be happy.

Without these two aspects, or with the absence or weakness of one of them, it will be very difficult for us to feel fulfilled, to procure a life of healthy relationships and to achieve a state of peace and tranquility with ourselves and, therefore, with the environment.

Self-esteem, both individual and collective, can be wounded at times, and then recover and create new models of thought on which a new consciousness is built or born. This can be expressed in individuals who overcome losses that were a considerable damage to their self-esteem, or in collectives or minorities, which have been marginalized from society for years, who then obtain important historical reparations, recognition or vindication. In both cases, we can speak of an evolution that brings with it reparation, the healing of the individual.

Throughout my experience as a therapist, I have seen, with astonishing recurrence, young people in their twenties or thirties in perfect health, as well as their partners, who came to me because of infertility. The first thing I look for in these people are the clues that lead me to the critical point from which it is no longer possible for them to create and sustain life.

Similarly, many situations of anxiety, fear, and guilt have their origin in family dynamics devoid of affection, characterized by the physical or emotional absence of the parents, or by an upbringing with excessive discipline and lack of acknowledgment of the emotional needs of the child. In any case, the losses in each of the patients, and their inability to elaborate them, have been the main cause of their decision to come to therapy.

I would like to share with you some of the experiences of patients, who managed to turn their lives around through deep self-knowledge and the courage to identify and transcend patterns of low self-esteem, which had dragged on for years, often at the limit of human pain and suffering, to the impoverishment of their life.

Margarita: the Feeling of Not Being Deserved

I was trying to get pregnant and had several miscarriages. We had been told that it would be impossible to have children naturally, so I had two artificial inseminations, both unsuccessful. I was very frustrated. The hormones made me very irritable and I told the doctor I wanted to stop. I was twenty-six and about to collapse. I decided to stop fertility treatment and wait a few months. During that time, a friend who had gone through the same thing told me about the COR Method and I started therapy.

At first, it was hard for me to talk about myself and I was surprised by the kind of questions Claudia asked me. Up to that point, I hadn't minded not having a religious or spiritual life. I am a biologist and I don't believe in anything that is not scientific.

In the first interview with Margarita, I was able to observe her great skepticism, which even led her to doubt science itself. After many attempts, in which she was unable to get pregnant naturally, and after two losses, she decided to give herself permission to go to therapy. Margarita's level of consciousness was one of great suffering and she was going through a process of discouragement from which she did not know how to get out.

Fortunately, in most people, intuition, "the inner doctor" referred to by Dr. John Upledger, prevails, leading them, after an important process of "surrender", to recognize that the physical problem contemplates complex aspects of the human being to which it is vital to listen and to treat. Margarita gradually awakened her courage and at one point asked herself the question: "How can I continue to live like this?"

> Claudia recommended the book *My Inner Physician and Me,* which I read in one sitting. It explained craniosacral therapy to people with a scientific mind. "Seeing is believing" has always been my motto. The book was written especially for people like me.

From an early age, Margarita's self-esteem was built around the pride of belonging to a lineage of eminent medics and, in this way, she learned to develop a scientific mind that for some time worked in an attempt to calm a nervous system that was always on the verge of collapse. She experienced life with very little joy. She had been taught that what was important, and where her security should rest, was the professional prestige of the family. Apart from this, she had a great immaturity that was expressed in her intimacy with her partner, full of taboos and puritanism. The subject of sexuality was distorted. Margarita recognized that there was no enjoyment and that coitus was only conceivable in terms of procreation.

> I stopped talking about fertility and babies and, without realizing it, I started a process of introspection. I started to focus on myself: how I saw my life, my childhood, my relationship. I started to look at my fears. I had never been to a psychologist before. It was like discovering myself for the first time.

In her case, craniosacral therapy was very effective in achieving somatic-emotional release, that is, getting in touch with her pain and giving another meaning to her experience. Many fears that were encapsulated emerged. The therapeutic conversation on the couch was crucial for her to realize where she was: full of insecurities, blockages, prejudices; a restricted mind. Through that subtle contact and dialogue with the body and body awareness, a process took place that allowed her to trust the therapy she was undergoing. However, there were times when she brought some situations that triggered her insecurity and she became blocked again. It took some time, but finally, Margarita began to disidentify herself from a constructed image behind which was her true essence.

Cognitive therapy proved very effective in undoing those convictions that were hindering any possibility of seeing and hearing herself.

> I was very closed-up and very uncommunicative about my feelings, about my emotions. I was removing layers, like peeling an onion, until I got to my deepest fears, to my experience as a daughter, to the emotional limitations I grew up with. I was full of fears, taboos and self-limitations.
>
> I became aware of the great fear of motherhood, of pain, of suffering for a loved one. I don't know anyone who hasn't had a fright with a child, who hasn't choked on a piece of candy, who hasn't broken a bone. Those thoughts tormented me. To make matters worse, at that time, I came across one of Claudia's patients who had lost her child in an accident.

Margarita was an example of an obsessive mind resulting from low self-esteem, which does not necessarily flourish in homes with wellbeing and structure. She did not feel deserving of happiness and thought and acted according to the unconscious dynamic of undeservedness.

She came to the office with several unprocessed grievances. Her not being able to get pregnant naturally nor through fertility treatments caused her a great loss of her sense of confidence. She did not trust her body to sustain life; she did not trust the sexual relationship by itself to procreate; she did not trust the feminine or the maternal, since her relationship with her mother was based on duty and not always on affection.

> I worked through a lot of relationship issues with my mom. I had an extremely strict and inflexible upbringing.

The information that emerged from the craniosacral therapy was that the relationship with her mother and, therefore, with the maternal in her, was severely affected. Let us take into account that the eggs are produced in the girl when she is still in her mother's womb. To this must be added how fundamental and necessary it is to close mourning in order to open up to life. She had lost contact with her own body and with the mechanisms she could not control. We worked weekly for a year building those key elements of self-esteem, such as the feeling of confidence and deservedness.

> One morning I went to visit a close childhood friend before leaving on a trip. When I arrived, I found her crying. She told me she was pregnant, but didn't know how to tell me. At that moment I did my best to bite my tongue and told her how happy I was for her. I cried all the way to the airport. It was very strange, as I had never, until that day, cried, and I couldn't stop crying. I told my husband, from the bottom of my heart, that if having a family wasn't for us, well, it wasn't going to be. I was so relieved to say it.
>
> That weekend I got pregnant. I had already made the decision that I was going to enjoy other things in my life, my youth, my marriage.

At this moment Margarita surrendered and was able to humbly open up to the possibility of seeing herself internally, which her low self-esteem was preventing her from doing. It was a beautiful awakening.

She had opened the door to joy and enjoyment. Moreover, she was able to recognize that she could not control everything. These two revelations allowed her to unburden herself through a very deep cry that had been silenced for a long time. Finally, she could allow herself not to be perfect in order to be loved and respected. For years, she lived out the demands and what should be, and now she was simply experiencing, for the first time in her life, that feeling of being worthy of happiness. Fortunately, self-esteem is a great repairer of our cells as well.

Roberto: the Anxiety of the Unwanted Child

> Living with my father was never easy. He was a very hard, rigid and strict person with me. I was born when he was sixty years old. There was a very wide generation gap. He was almost a grandfather, not a loving grandfather, but unnecessarily harsh. This tension between us still persists.
>
> The COR Method allowed me to identify the emotions that made me anxious. It wasn't easy; it isn't a job that can be done overnight because it requires a lot of honesty with oneself and it removes a lot of pain.

Low self-esteem and anxiety are closely related to the primary rejection he was subjected to when he was conceived. Roberto was an unwanted child who did not receive the affection, recognition and acceptance that a human being needs to develop a robust ego structure. The family, as the child's first nucleus of interaction, failed in its role. This feeling has not only accompanied him throughout his life, but has conditioned an insecure, distrustful and anxious personality. His vision of life has been marked by undeservedness, which has generated chronic anxiety that detonates and provokes crises in the face of the challenges he must necessarily experience.

His despair must have been great for him to make the decision to open up the way he did in therapy. It was an act of honesty for him to acknowledge his attempts at self-harm in response to life's challenges, as well as to verbalize his feelings of low self-esteem. Roberto was living in hiding behind a hostile façade, which concealed a great deal of unspoken, but self-flagellating inner rage. He had the confidence to open up to express his emotions. The work consisted in being able to say with conviction: "I am worth it". But to do so, he first had to regain a sense of confidence.

> I have been a tennis player since I was eight years old. I participated, representing my country, in numerous international open tennis tournaments. I was always surrounded by sports psychologists, but working with them was very different. We made lists to identify where I was going; lists of the things I had as ambitions; lists of the goals I had achieved and the causes of my failures; they would make me reflect and write down the reasons why I thought I had not been able to reach my goals. They stayed more on the subject of performance. Although we did breathing and relaxation exercises.
>
> I knew internally that this was not enough. Then the tremors started, and as they became more frequent and intense, I knew I had to get to the root of the problem. The issue then was that I didn't know how or where to start. I went to a neurologist and had tests done. The diagnosis was sports stress, but I knew there was more to it.

I received specialized therapy to avoid hand tremors. Research on the internet became my life. I went through everything, I tried everything.

To my surprise, Claudia's therapy did not focus on the tremor problem. We started with craniosacral therapy. She was talking about anxiety, not tremors.

As I began to see results, I opened up a little more, because I am usually very reserved. We started to look into aspects that I had never been aware of before. I realized why my anxiety was manifesting itself.

Trust is the starting point for any therapy. Trust in the therapist, but also in oneself and in the way the process unfolds. For me, each therapy, every patient that comes to my office is an act of faith. Faith in their possibilities and in the power of self-repair of the human psyche.

I could see my lack of self-esteem, of self-confidence. The trembling came in moments of extreme anguish when I needed to do something well to receive recognition. Now, though I knew it, I thought I still couldn't attack it.

Although Roberto was very aware of his wounds of abandonment and psychological havoc as the sequelae of affective neglect, until he verbalized it in therapy, he could not consciously decide to take responsibility for his process. He began to value himself. From that moment on, we were able to go deeper.

I am back to tennis. No longer professionally, but as a hobby. The tremor has diminished by 80%, I dare say. I feel very confident and enthusiastic. I travel a lot and, although Claudia is currently not in the country, we have continued the online therapy. It is a process that has to be continuous to be effective. It is like a fracture that needs months in a cast to heal.

This phrase describes and summarizes very well the emotional repair of his psyche.

> I can't believe that, until just a year ago, in addition to the tremors, I also had a tightness in my chest and felt like I was drowning. Such was the anxiety I was suffering from. I took anxiolytics for a long time and I needed more and more.
>
> Now I am convinced that diseases must be cured from the inside out. From their real causes and not just attacking the symptoms. It may take more time; it is not the shortest or easiest way, but it is the only effective one.
>
> I am much more aware of my destructive thoughts, of the fears I have, of the little confidence in myself and in others. I have been able to see it. Of course, we live in a country where it is difficult not to be afraid. But, in my case, I feed those fears. Especially in personal relationships. I am afraid that they are going to hurt me.
>
> The change has not only been relief of my physical symptoms, but in my character. I notice it and everyone notices it, my family, my co-workers. I have more confidence in what I do, and in the future. I am more optimistic. I don't question things as much. I feel more confident, more open, I can talk. If I don't like something, I am able to say so and not swallow it.

The latter is very important because, in Roberto, there was an avoidance mechanism known as retroflection, by means of which, in his particular case, affective manifestations such as anger, instead of channeling them externally, he directed them towards himself. Quoting Dr. Guillermo Feo[18], retroflection has two modalities that involve "doing to oneself what one would like to do to the other [...] or doing to oneself what one would like another to do to him [...] In neither case is there satisfaction, only frustration and regret".

Part of the therapy with Claudia, in addition to the online therapeutic conversations, is meditation. The truth is that I don't know what I am saying in the mantra, but it works! The chanting relaxes me and I begin to feel a rare peace I have never felt before.

Before coming to consultation, Roberto became interested in meditation and began to practice it daily. I think that this courage to assume his vulnerability and work on his anxiety came from a state of surrender and acceptance to which the practitioner is led through meditation.

Today, Roberto has been able to rebuild his self-esteem despite having suffered injuries to the depths of his psyche. He has been in a stable relationship for a year and a half and is expecting his first child.

At a certain point, the way he began to tell his life story took a turn, thanks to which it was now possible to give value to his life experience.

Brigitte: the Value of Being Authentic

I met my husband at the age of twenty-two at a time when my life made a break, both family and social spheres. This marked a before and after because I was living in Disneyland. My family was involved in a big financial scandal in Colombia that made headlines in the national press.

I remember that at the time I thought everything was at my feet; I was very conceited and self-centered. I was focused only on my social life, parties, traveling, and suddenly I got that jolt.

After the scandal, we continued to meet the same people, in the same places, but we no longer had any contact. We lost many of our so-called friends.

I suffered a lot, but I didn't believe that I could fall into depression as I had seen other people close to me do. I thought that, because of the way I am, that would never happen to me, but yes, I fell into depression and decided to seek help.

Brigitte, a young Colombian woman from a well-off family, came to my office in a state of deep sadness, feeling that her world had come to an end. The incident involving her father in a media scandal generated a deep crisis both at the family and individual levels. Brigitte's emotional security, her self-esteem, was based on very weak foundations, such as belonging to a social stratum and having an influential financial position. When the family setback occurred, when this false structure of belonging collapsed, everyone began to review and, therefore, to rebuild themselves.

A key aspect in Brigitte's process was the absence of integrity and authenticity in the social settings in which Brigitte and her family were involved. This resulted in an enormous lack of self-esteem. For this reason, the social isolation of the family, the consequent scandal and, even the formation of sides over the event, were so shocking and traumatic. The value of this cultural sphere is that money makes me: "I am as long as I have".

Whether it is an ordinary person with a simple and seemingly insignificant story, a big celebrity, or a person who has lived through a war or a unique trauma, integrity and authenticity are key to an individual's ability to take ownership of his or her destiny.

One of the most important and difficult existential processes of the individual is to recognize his own lack of integrity. It involves a great deal of honesty in order to be able to see oneself. Integrity is understood here as the attribute of completeness that a human being possesses, according to how well he or she has assumed his or her luminous facets and his or her shadows. From this point of view, there is no conflict or contradiction between what one believes, what one thinks and how one acts. It is a matter of being authentic, which implies being consistent, accepting oneself and showing oneself as one is.

> My parents also sought help. I was trying to find answers and one of the things I learned is that, in situations like these, there are always two truths or two perceptions of what really happened: yours and the others'.

Brigitte began to see her own shortcomings through what was happening in her family. When we are able to see the other, we can integrate those aspects that are not the same as our own. They needed to see each other in order to expand their life maps.

> I remember perfectly well when I entered the office. Claudia led me to the couch and started craniosacral therapy. When she touched my legs, she asked me: "What is going on in your family?
> At that moment I started to cry. I was suffering from pains in my legs, they were swelling up. I had already visited several doctors.

What sustains us, what connects us to the earth, the ultimate security — and that is the family — is located in the legs. When the family nucleus is in crisis, this is reflected in the legs. The legs support us and move us and the hands allow us to grasp, to hold on. These are elemental aspects of self-esteem.

> Craniosacral therapy helped me manage the physical pain, as well as the pain I felt emotionally. Little by little I accepted that we lived in an unreal world where everything was a fantasy. In my family, we lived a lot by what people would say. We belonged to a circle in which we all acted like a herd. It was a very painful awakening, but now I understand that it was necessary. The situation made us all change.

This crisis was undoubtedly the catalyst that led Brigitte to confront herself, her family and her social environment.

To be whole and authentic, we have to make room for our fears and insecurities. Make them part of us. We only consider the search for integrity and authenticity when we begin to ask ourselves, who am I? When self-esteem is low, we try to hide those aspects for which we believe we will not be accepted.

> Therapy with the COR Method went through several stages, first craniosacral, then Gestalt, therapeutic conversations, workshops and, in a more recent phase, we have begun to include meditations, which I now do on my own and have included in my daily routine.

It is really very comforting to see Brigitte's evolution over time and how she has taken more responsibility in her process.

> I could have stayed in anger or victimized myself without getting over it. My therapy was to discover who I am and what I want to do with my life. I worked a lot on overcoming the fear of being found out that I am not perfect; on learning to

recognize my pain; on accepting myself; on forgiving others and on forgiving myself.

I continue my therapies, now online, because I continue to grow; it is a constant process in which new challenges appear. I strongly believe in the importance of investing time, energy and resources in mental health, just as we do with bodily health.

I want to raise my child with emotional intelligence and, above all, resilience. In this changing world, it is vital to develop the ability to adapt permanently.

Finally, I understood that the important thing is to focus on changing internally rather than trying to change external circumstances. I am more aware of the transformation I am undergoing, as well as that of my family. Are we going to allow an internet algorithm to know us better than we know ourselves?

In Brigitte's process we can see how her life began to be more assertive from a healed self-esteem. She has come to terms with herself just as she is, living without the conditioning factors of the world in which she grew up. She has humbly decided to be more integral, more authentic, and this decision has transformed her into a more serene, more self-confident person. She is on the most important path that any person can start. It is a very painful process, which involves giving up everything that was previously defended as part of oneself. Her commitment to her personal growth is total, which makes me have great faith in her and her process.

Fernando: Success as a Facade

Fernando is a young, very self-confident businessman from Medellin. Life seems to smile at him: a brilliant degree, graduated with honors; married to a beautiful woman from Cali, who is also a businesswoman; father of three children; and founder of one of the most important transportation companies in Colombia. By the standards of our modern society, we wouldn't hesitate to define him as a successful man.

He decided to go to consultation due to a crisis that detonated in his work environment and led him to relive painful unresolved family events that needed to be addressed without further delay.

> My family environment was quite peculiar. My parents, both divorced and with children from their ex-partners, remarried, but had decided not to have any more children. Soon the disagreements between them began, which worsened with my arrival in this world. Over the years I realized that I had been born in the midst of a conflict and that this had definitely marked my life. I have been analyzing the facts deeply, tying up ends. Perhaps that is why I always act as a mediator. That seems to be the fate of my life, to be in the middle of a problem, trying to avoid conflict. All the time I am trying to reconcile positions; to avoid problems: in the family, between partners, in everything. It's very tiring.

Fernando came to therapy with a level of consciousness situated in a very marked egocentrism that, in reality, hides a deep pain and a need to act according to duty over and above his own desires. In him there is an abysmal separation, an enormous distance between his ideal and his true self.

Fernando has an aversion to conflict, avoids it and, when it is imminent, uses everything to silence it and tries to get things back to normal. To what he believes should be normality, understood as the absence of chaos or conflict. Thus, he lives divided between his ideal self and what he really is.

In fact, Fernando is trapped in the "should be" and does everything possible with the resources he possesses not to touch that fear that paralyzes him. Gifted with a great intelligence, he has managed to intellectualize his pain; but it is not possible for him to experience it, to feel it. There is still a lot of resistance in him. He lives in analysis and his greatest difficulty is not having been able to elaborate the mourning of his birth and a childhood lacking affection.

Up to this point in therapy, while he has made some changes, his structure is still very rigid and he continues to be stuck in it.

Eight years ago, when I had a work problem and was very tense, someone recommended the COR Method, developed by Claudia. I was feeling very tired physically and emotionally. As usual, I was between two waters: a friend and my partners. I was either the good guy with one or with the other. The fact is that after I had arrived at the session and lay down on the couch for the craniosacral therapy, she touched my feet and immediately asked me about my father. I was very surprised. Later I learned that the relationship with the father is associated with the feet, as they are the base.

I was able to work in therapy on many unfinished aspects of that first conflictive relationship with my father, but, in my particular case, I felt that the necessary acceptance to be able to heal this type of family relationship came to me through the practice of meditation.

I didn't go to therapy for a while. Then we had a crisis when our first child was born. My wife's family is a bit reminiscent of the one in the movie *My Big Fat Greek Wedding:* they are intense, they know no boundaries, and it was very difficult for them to respect our privacy as a couple and as parents. I, being a survivor of a family with an older, distant dad and an absent mom, could hardly tolerate what I considered an invasion. We began to have disagreements because they saw the baby every day and showered him with gifts and knick-knacks. I didn't want to raise my son like that. My wife felt I was attacking her and it was very difficult to make her understand my reasons. We went to three sessions and understood the differences in the families, with different roles, but with the same goals.

My first experience with meditation began when I became associated with a company where one of the partners had introduced a corporate meditation program for his employees. I remember being very surprised to see five hundred people meditating at the same time; even more so in Medellin, where there is a strong religious and family tradition. This changed my life. When I told Claudia about it, she was very interested and, finally, ended up restructuring the meditation program for the company.

Subsequently, I did a thirty-hour meditation workshop with my wife. For two weekends in a row, just the two of us. There we discovered many things about each other. In those sessions, the problem with my father, which hurt me so much, came back to me and I could see many patterns in my behavior that were conditioned by that relationship. I decided to incorporate meditation as part of my daily routine.

Last year we did a meditation program with twenty-five company employees. A total of twelve hours of work in one weekend. The results were not long in coming. Many of the employees started meditating on their own after that experience. The company did a 180-degree turn and even many of the people who participated in this pilot test told us that their own families were experiencing major changes in the way they related to each other. There was a case of a man who began to cry during the meditation, because he had left a lot of things unresolved with his father, who had recently passed away. As a result of this experience, his relationship with his third son, which had been very complicated, began to improve considerably. There were many similar testimonies, but I remember that one in particular because of my personal issue.

The change in the office was noticeable in employees' relationships with their families and among co-workers. Attention to work increased. The atmosphere became more sensitive, more human. A person from the COR Method team was following up with them. Measurements showed us that the error rate and stress level had dropped in a very short time.

At first there was some resistance because there is a lot of ignorance and myths surrounding meditation, but after that Saturday, everything changed. One employee told me that meditation was his motivation to go to work.

Now I know that in order to identify the root of my problems, I needed silence. In the midst of the hectic life I was leading, it would have been impossible. It was like taking a huge burden off my back that I didn't know I was carrying, but that wouldn't let me walk. My relationship with my father had changed, though he probably didn't even realize it. I finally understood that he was not going to change, that what I had to do was to accept him as he was, without conditions, and change my perception of the relationship. There was no time to lose.

A very valuable lesson I have learned from all this is that we are not the product of external circumstances, but of the decisions we make in relation to those circumstances.

What is the most important thing for me, then? Knowing that I can't control what happens outside. I am learning to let go of the things that are not in my control. That has given me much more peace of mind and energy to focus on the things I can intervene in. It is clearer to me than ever that we cannot waste our energy in wanting to have control over everything and in having expectations that only generate frustration.

All this has led me to have greater sensitivity and compassion for myself and those around me. Now I feel a great longing to share the experience I have learned. I started creating a WhatsApp group with the young people in the family, to pass on information about spiritual matters. Both my wife and I have awakened to a sense of wanting to do something for others. Two years ago, I didn't have that awareness, I just wanted to work, grow as an entrepreneur and make money. Now we have that responsibility that has become a life purpose.

When I was doing my research to implement corporate meditation, I was pleasantly surprised to learn that companies, such as Mitsubishi, or institutions, such as the Canadian Police, had been doing it for years. In some schools around the world, meditation is a fixed activity from an early age.

His work in the company is also based on his duty self. He has built an image of himself as a progressive businessman. He would like to be progressive.

I trust that Fernando's great intelligence will allow him to continue to break down the barriers that prevent him from fully expressing his desired self. I hope I can witness that journey into his inner self to discover the great man he is.

Elisa: the White Sheep. When the Family Doesn't Help...

My dad fell out with his family when I was born and lost his job. That was all I knew and I, in my naivety, couldn't help but think that maybe it was my fault. My relationship with him was always good. He would take me hunting and fishing. But my father was a person with many frustrations. He never resolved them. He hated his mom and dad. He had a lot of problems because of his anger. He died of stomach cancer.

I always said I preferred my dad to my mom. When I was little, I liked to be with her, but later I didn't. I wondered why she never helped me, why she didn't pay attention to me, why she didn't take care of me.

When I was twelve, I went to live with my aunt. And from then on, I felt an immense relief. My family environment was not easy at all. It was a very problematic environment, I thought that sooner or later I was going to get sick too. Everything was so toxic.

From Elisa's testimony, we can extract the importance of the family environment as the first affective nucleus of the human being, which is a determining factor in the construction of self-esteem. Elisa, as she describes it, was born into a family in which practically all its members suffered from some kind of disorder. Nevertheless, or quite happily, Elisa showed signs of being a lucid young woman, with a healthy psyche, who came to my office because of an unprocessed depression caused by a feeling of abandonment that had accompanied her from an early age. Fortunately, an aunt assumed her support and care.

I never had much of a relationship with my paternal family until my father got sick. The reconciliation was very nice. I never understood how he could change so suddenly. From having such a bad temper, he became very loving despite the hard times.

My dad was a brilliant economist. He was like an encyclopedia: he knew everything. However, I would have wanted him to be a psychologist. Maybe then he would have been able to work through all those contradictory emotions that tormented him so much.

But now I understand that everyone has their own story and that's why we have to try to forgive. I try to forgive my mom for her absences. I always felt strange. I wondered why I didn't have a family like other girls. I have a lot of friends and I love them dearly. When I was little, I had a very close friend, but one day we had a fight and I felt very lonely. I remember I went to Claudia and we talked about it at length. At first, I suffered a lot. I had low self-esteem and still do, but as a child, I was even worse. I did things all the time to please my friends. Sometimes I gave them all my money and I was left with nothing. I was lonely. With Dad's illness, I grew up a lot. I had to be well to be able to help him.

By the time Elisa came to therapy, she had a highly idealized image of her father, who, although angry and later ill, maintained a close relationship with his daughter. Elisa's lack of emotional contact with her mother, as a consequence of the latter's psychological disorder, created in Elisa, the youngest child, a deep feeling of rejection and abandonment that significantly damaged her security and self-esteem.

As a typical adolescent with a troubled home, Elisa also idealized other families and clung to her friends, so much so that she was influenced by them in order to be accepted. The social environment becomes very important during adolescence and in Elisa's case led her to develop some phobias.

After several sessions with the young woman, I wanted to make sure that her low self-esteem was due more to environmental causes than to some disorder possibly inherited or imitated from her family. Moreover, this was one of Elisa's great fears: to suffer from the family's disease or for it to reoccur in her at some point.

The results of the psychiatric study cleared up her doubts and gave her peace of mind.

This was the moment to start a process of elaboration of all the wounds, to rebuild the notion of a broken family in which the maternal aunt seemed to be the only one who gave any structure to the young girl.

> When my dad got sick, I wondered why him, and not my mom, who has so many food problems and is not a healthy person. I also wondered why these things were happening to me. Why do I have the mom I have? With therapy, you work on those thoughts and the feelings they generate in order to overcome them. When you manage to internalize it, you even become grateful for those "bad things", because of the teachings you received. You stop worrying so much.
>
> In the end you see how all the pieces fit together, everything has its reason. I would like to be a better person and help others to be happy. But, above all, I would like to get rid of this feeling of abandonment I have because of my mother. When I came home from school, she was sleeping. I felt and still feel her absence very much. Sometimes I feel that mom doesn't think and react the same way as other human beings. It affects me a lot. I try to understand her without judging her.

Elisa suffered from persecution delirium and phobias. There was a latent risk, even though she was a healthy person, that at any moment a psychotic condition could awaken in her and she could go down the family path. Therapy rescued her at a decisive moment when she was ready to work out how she came into this world and into a family like hers. In the midst of chaos and a great crisis, it was urgent to structure who she was and her role in that family picture. We dedicated many hours of work on the structuring of her self, to her self-perception and to the recognition of her innermost fears.

When I feel bad, I try to reflect and be grateful for what I have. I make an effort every day to be and feel good. Physical exercise helps me a lot. When I finished high school, I thought about studying psychology, but then I thought better of it. I wanted to do something different with my life, something that would excite me more. I have always been with psychologists since I was a child.

In spite of everything, I hope I never get into a fight with my family like my dad did, and if that were to happen, I would like to be able to put pride aside, forgive and ask for forgiveness. You have to sit down with each other. Communication is important. My mom had a lot of resentment towards Dad's family. And I would tell her that she should forgive too. She still has a hard time. I've realized what is essential, what is really valuable, and what happens in a moment of life and death. I remember that my dad got along the worst with his younger brother. When he went to visit him at the clinic, my dad wouldn't let him leave.

When I came to Claudia, I started with craniosacral therapy and then continued with meditation and therapeutic conversations.

I still meditate, I try to do it every day. Claudia taught me. It helps me a lot. There's a big difference between the days I meditate and the days I don't. Like 180 degrees. Meditation helps me have the day I want to have. I always conclude with a feeling of gratitude in my heart.

Once, my aunt went on a trip and I tried to call her several times, but I couldn't get through. I felt very bad because she did not answer me right away. I felt that she was not looking out for me. I was in a very bad mood. It was very hard for me to accept that a family member did not call me or that I could not talk to a friend at a given moment. I felt completely abandoned. Now I am aware that this feeling came from maternal abandonment. I worked a lot on that in therapy.

And suddenly, after a while, without even realizing it, I saw the change in me. I started to accept and forgive. It's like magic.

With Elisa, we can speak therapeutically of a successful experience in a short time. In her story, we can see how she became aware of her process. A sixteen-year-old adolescent who was able to elaborate on having an absent paternal family, a sick sister, a depressive mother, and an angry father who became ill and died.

Her ability to visualize, to project herself into the future was a great help. Elisa could have escaped into drugs or any other addiction coming from such a toxic family, but she managed to save herself from that hostile environment thanks to an important process of elaboration. Likewise, her mental organization and ability to focus enabled her to get into a prestigious American university and graduate. She was able to connect with her healthy mind and from there obtain the tools to work on herself.

Elisa's aunt, a woman with a strict religious upbringing, always tried to make Elisa seek the necessary consolation for her reality of life in the Church. However, despite her youth, Elisa was always able to discern between the dogmatic and the spiritual. At all times she showed great awareness of what a therapeutic process entailed, and, although she was not the one who paid the cost of the sessions, her commitment was total. Although Elisa was born and raised in a pre-psychotic family, she possessed great emotional intelligence, which is not very common in adolescents.

Her great learning was to be able to work through the unresolved experiences that caused her so much suffering.

I think she would have been a very good artist, but her aunt was very influential in her choice of a financial career in order to take over the family business in absence of other relatives who could do so.

Chapter 9
Non-consciousness of Illness

I read some statements made by the Spanish writer Rosa Montero to the *Babelia* journalist, Silvia Hernando, in the article "Memories of discomfort", published in the newspaper *El País*, on June 4: "2021 was the year in which, due to the pandemic, mental disorders in the world came out of the closet [...] the taboo could no longer be maintained". And I could not agree more with that statement. We are living in an era that tends to shed light on issues that used to be hidden, and mental health is certainly one of them.

As a therapist, I have talked at length with my colleagues about how traumatic this experience has been and about the fact that, nevertheless, we have had to go through this collective trauma to become aware of the problems that many of us already had and that, because we had not dealt with them on time, they came up in an evident and inescapable way.

Another of the many reflections I can draw from personal experience is that, despite all the technological advances, and the welfare society we have been able to create, our psyche is still fragile and in many cases incapable of handling unexpected situations of sustained stress and anxiety. This should necessarily lead us to rethink our indicators of progress, to prioritize above all the most important resource we have: the mind, and through it the way we perceive the world and the resources it creates to respond to the challenges of life.

It would seem that, in this new phase of human evolution, the task ahead of us as a species is to balance the energy consumed by the mind in creating increasingly efficient technological societies and to use that same energy in ourselves, in making our mind a true instrument in the service of human evolution.

It is interesting to observe how in some societies the fact of going to therapy is seen as something absolutely normal; on the contrary, in others, this fact is avoided and, unless there is no other choice, it is hidden, since it brings shame to both the person and his or her relatives. There are individuals who instinctively seek to reach a state of mind from which to increase their capacity for discernment, to distinguish perception from reality, or to recognize traumatic situations that have left their mark. Others are forced to do so by the disease itself. The important thing here is to understand that life will subtly or crudely introduce the changes we need in order to evolve.

Throughout my professional experience, I have seen the cruelest face of the disease: psychotic outbreaks, suicides... This time, the individual has reached collective dimensions. Society is increasingly collapsing because it does not have the necessary tools to process events of great emotional, physical and existential intensity. Some countries have begun to sound the alarms of public mental health, others are trying to go further and have begun to understand the urgent need for a change in our paradigms, habits and ways of relating to our environment.

In the various workshops and courses in which I participated as part of my training in meditation techniques, both in India and in Portugal, the monks explained to us their vision according to which, in the face of unbearable pain, the psyche of the individual will tend to take one of three paths: to not continue living, to connect with the mystical-spiritual or to lose the sense of reality. The last one is the most common way out in our society today.

One of the main challenges before starting therapy is the absence of awareness of the disease or disorder or condition in the patient. A person who comes to therapy aware that there is something to heal, who is handled with extreme discretion by their family, work-social circle for fear of stigma, is not the same as a person who comes looking for quick or timely solutions to issues that have their origin in a condition or disorder unrecognized or denied in themselves.

Denial of illness, both physical and mental, may be, at first, the healthy mechanism of a mind that needs to process information that is painful, stressful, or that threatens its sense of security and exposes its vulnerability. The problem arises when that denial translates into resistance and interferes with the therapeutic process.

Denial comes from lack of self-knowledge and the biggest obstacle will always be ignorance. Greater investment in mental health education is required. The risk of a condition turning into a disease is always latent, and thus it will be conceived and develop. Alcohol, drugs and other narcotics accelerate these processes. Hence the importance of focusing our attention on environmental contexts and, in this sense, the family environment plays a preponderant role.

Becoming aware of the disease is a family and social process, so ideally the therapist needs to involve the parents, or the partner, or the children, so that this environment provides a favorable space, free of judgments and even false diagnoses due to lack of information or knowledge. Most of the time mental pathology is suffered alone, which can further isolate the individual and aggravate the condition.

Once the disease is established, it is difficult to make contact with the patient. Safeguards such as anger are a valuable opportunity for the therapist since it is the way the patient finds to relate to his environment.

Apart from family factors, there are other social variables that can play a fundamental role in the process of acquiring awareness of the disease which have a greater impact on people with low financial resources. The costs of therapy are usually high, since they are weekly sessions and sometimes even several times a week, and Social Security does not usually cover this type of care, which jeopardizes the continuity of treatment. In addition, many health systems offer the patient medication more than talking therapies, which generates drug dependency. There are also emergency telephone lines, but, once again, assistance operates from the immediacy of assisting a crisis.

There is another equally unfavorable reality and, in this case, it affects people with families who have the necessary resources to pay for psychological or psychiatric assistance: the family's fear that the patient may become dependent on the therapist or, even worse, that the therapist may "stir things up" and threaten the family codes or jeopardize precarious family stability.

Deny and Hide: Nothing Happens...

Belen, a woman from Madrid, was born into a very Catholic and conservative family that came from a town in Leon. She had a rather austere early childhood, a situation that changed with her father's financial progress, which allowed a rapid social ascent for the family. Belen was always aware of the enormous intellectual difference that existed between her father and her mother, and also that she did not want to resemble her older sister, a girl with Attention Deficit Disorder, who caused so much concern to her parents.

> I was born in Madrid forty-three years ago; I was the second of four sisters and grew up in a structured and happy family. As much was expected of me, I was always studious and I got good grades; I was never a problem child. I was chubby and suffered what would now be called bullying by some kids, but I had personality and character and didn't let it seem to affect me, although it did take its toll. I went to endocrinologists, went on diets, lost a lot of weight and became very pretty — boys started to like me a lot. As I didn't want to be fat again, I suffered episodes of bulimia; my parents, at a certain point, seemed to notice, but only slightly. I never went for treatment or anything, I knew how to hide it well. I was a reserved child. I rarely shared my fears and concerns so as not to worry my parents. Despite these little things, I grew up happy and my parents were proud of me.

Belen minimizes the disorder of bulimia and acknowledges that she has never been treated. Most bulimics are female, adolescent, and belong to higher socioeconomic groups. Clinical evidence shows that, in most cases, adolescents who develop bulimia come from families with mental health problems, such as affective disorders. It is common for adolescents with bulimia to have other mental health problems, such as anxiety disorders or emotional disorders. The symptoms of bulimia can be similar to those of other psychiatric conditions or medical problems. Belen, like many other young women with this disorder, initially kept her illness hidden and very private.

The comment "my parents seemed to notice, but only slightly" suggests that the entire nuclear family was in denial or unaware of the mental health disorder. She finishes by saying that, except for those "little things", she grew up happy. Likewise, Belen, with great intelligence as a child, sensed that her parents could do little for her. Her mother was preoccupied with her troubled sister; and her father, busy with work, was totally oblivious to his family's emotional needs. It is difficult to determine the cause of bulimia. In Belen's case, several factors are present, including cultural ideals and newly adopted social attitudes: appearance, self-evaluation and family problems of adapting to the environment. Recognizing rejection for being chubby, or because she was a newcomer to the school she was able to attend due to the family's socioeconomic advancement, led her to believe that there was something wrong with her. She decided to lose weight and become an attractive young woman, to be the best student, the exemplary daughter, whatever it took not to be rejected. She also decided to carry all that anxiety and suffering in silence and hide it out of shame.

> I studied Administration because my father worked as an administrator and for convenience. I think I was not brave and, now from a distance, I was afraid of choosing a career in which I could not succeed and would disappoint... I also liked Law and I would have done Judiciary, but I think I thought I would not be able to... I worked in several companies, but I have always been very disappointed with the bosses I have had; I would have loved to have a boss like my father, to admire and learn from.

The need to identify herself with her father, whom Belen admired, and not with her mother, made the young girl set herself the task of fitting in and being accepted —first by her father, then by her high society companions with whom she now alternated— by not causing problems, "getting by" alone so as not to worry anyone as they already had enough to worry about with her sister. Her self-esteem was strongly shaken and her emotional world had to be suffocated so that she could conceal the enormous tension and suffering that this generated in her.

> I don't talk to my mother much, and if I do, it's mostly to get my mind off my worries and fears. She is a wonderful and kind woman, but she is one of those people who get on my nerves. Besides, after having always been her shoulder to cry on, her help, her shield and her support, I have not felt very supported and protected by her, which is why I do not talk about many things… I'm sure she will say that I am like my father.

Although there was no pathology in terms of mental health, Belen developed an identity conflict that had a lot to do with the acceptance of her body, and with the search for the maternal ideal in toxic female friendships in which she was always in competition. With her mother, there was a double bind. First, she turned little Belen into her comforter and demanded that she become an adult before her time in order to console her over the condition of her sister, who was totally dependent on her parents. An emotional abuse came about, which the daughter was unwilling to perpetuate. On the other hand, the mother resented the rejection of the daughter, who ignored her because she could not feel admiration for her. Belen, in identifying with her father who was oblivious to the affective needs of the family members and in the search for acceptance and security that only he could provide, suffocated her emotions because she was ashamed to show her vulnerability. She decided to live in a world of performance, achieved goals, and professional success at the expense of her own feelings.

> I met Claudia by chance, at a conference she was giving in Madrid on self-esteem. At that time, I had a lot of doubts about

how I was raising my daughters and how to deal with certain issues. My main goal is for them to be happy.

Belen came to my office worried about her older daughter's anxiety states, which produced a strong fear of death and panic attacks. She came to ask for help for her daughter. What she could not do for herself, she was now doing for her daughter. At that moment, she was not yet ready to see her own fears, her own anxiety, after long years of training to hide her suffering.

> That was the starting point, I began face-to-face therapy with Claudia to address the issues of my child that concerned me, but soon the therapy began to focus more on me: on my lack of self-esteem, perhaps due to my childhood body complexes, and my obsessive need to fit in and not be a problem for anyone. I really liked that Claudia was a foreigner and that she was not known in my immediate circle. That assured me that I wouldn't have to bump into anyone in the office. I didn't tell anyone. I paid cash for my sessions so that there would be no trace on my bank statement. Afterwards, I was fine with online therapy: with her being far away, it gave me a sense of peace of mind knowing that no one would find out. There are still a lot of taboos about going to therapy; mental health and emotional education from an early age have not been addressed. I still don't dare to talk freely about these issues.

As she began therapy with her daughter, Belen began to recognize her own process and was able to see how all those emotions that she had spent years believing she had under control, because no one suspected them, she had transferred to her daughter. She learned from a very young age to hide even from herself. It was very important for Belen to get in touch with her own process in order to be able to help her daughter. Before coming to my office, she confessed to me that she was in a state of absolute denial from which it was impossible for her to accept what other child therapists were telling her. She thought that if she had overcome everything on her own, her daughter could too, without anyone's help.

> The COR Method therapy helped me a lot to know myself; to see aspects that I was denying in myself, which somehow my daughters were manifesting in anxiety states. I have been able to see clearly how I assumed my sensitivity as something that had to be hidden and replaced by good grades and by an excellent performance at work. I understood that this was the way to connect with my father and not let him down. I have been able to resolve many of the concerns I brought to therapy the first time. However, the issue of my vocation, of my true purpose in life, I still cannot resolve. Perhaps it's because of the closeness with my father, on whose approval I still depend a lot. All this new awareness has helped me to let my sensitivity emerge, to forgive myself for what I considered as mistakes, to reconcile myself with imperfection, to accept myself more as I am, and not as I would like to be seen.

In the midst of her process, Belen allowed herself to explore her own sexuality through an extramarital experience, outside her comfort zone. Far from feeling guilt or fear, she began to ask herself questions and find answers about her identity, which had been blurred in the course of her life story.

Belen today, as an adult, has been able to become aware of how she spent years hiding her emotions out of shame and hiding her needs so as not to become a problem for others, as well as her terrible fear of rejection. It was very important to strengthen her self-esteem, and see her own process in therapy, by recognizing all that she had achieved in life: being financially independent, becoming a successful and attractive woman, choosing her life partner wisely, starting a beautiful family, and taking care of her children's mental health. Likewise, as she experienced for herself the challenges that motherhood entails, she also reconciled with her mother's image and was able to recognize her worth.

Her great intelligence, cultivated since she was a child, is what has allowed her to make good decisions throughout her life. This is what we know as evolutionary intelligence.

> I want the family I have formed to be better than mine. I will use all my resources to make this family that I have founded healthier and happier than the family I came from.

Chapter 10
The COR Method and the Challenges of the 21st Century

Since long before working from home was imposed on our lives by COVID-19, I have been familiar and very comfortable with online therapies. The contingency presented to us by the pandemic added to the previous process I have been going through, has allowed me to test and reinforce the COR Method, especially in the online setting.

From 2012-2014, I did some therapeutic courses at a university located in the south of India. We did some hard face-to-face work that we continued to deepen online when we returned to our countries. It seemed incredible to me that the same thing I experienced in India I could experience at home via Zoom. This university was one of the pioneers in using this modality to continue contact with their students, as well as to reach a wider audience that was not planning to travel to India. They decide to hold workshops in auditoriums all over the world with audiences of up to five hundred people. This made me realize that geographical or physical distance was not a limitation for therapeutic contact and follow-up. So, I decided to try it with my patients, not only with those who had emigrated, but also with those who lived far away and had difficulties crossing the city to get to the sessions on time. Of course, many people showed resistance to this new technological alternative.

Thus, the virtual work experience of the last few years trained me to anticipate a technological world that was already becoming part of our lives. It has also been a magnificent preparation, which has allowed me to continue with my activity without having to incorporate significant changes or adaptations to my work and study routine. It has given me greater flexibility to manage my schedule and to treat my patients when they or I are traveling; I am always available wherever I am.

In this sense, the COR Method has been able to update its fundamental tools to help individuals in their personal growth, integral health and well-being through individual workshops that require a sustained commitment of approximately fifty hours. The idea is to work with greater focus and depth in the individual processes of each person and identify the obstacles to transcend them. This is how we have created four fundamental pillars of therapeutic work:

1. Self-sabotage.
2. Self-esteem.
3. Awakening to other levels of consciousness.
4. Meditation.

Based on these pillars, we have developed tools to respond to the needs of people who perhaps haven't been to therapy before, because they considered that they did not have any specific problem to solve, although they were aware that they needed to work on some aspects to improve their relationships, health or some situations in their lives that were not going the way they wanted. These tools in the form of workshops also help these people to become sensitized and "lose their fear" of going to therapy.

The workshop on **Self-sabotage**, at a first level, is aimed at identifying the emotions that accompany each level of consciousness, as well as the causes and behaviors that keep us stuck in comfort zones that prevent the achievement of our goals or desires. Self-sabotage is an unconscious mechanism that manifests itself in various forms, from fear to laziness or excuses for not taking responsibility for our own lives.

The **Self-esteem** workshop is at a more advanced level. The image you have of yourself will determine what your life experience will be. Destiny depends on the perception you have of yourself. If I have a poor self-image, my level of self-esteem will be very low and my destiny will be chaos. This workshop is designed to understand why self-esteem is essential in our lives and more so in these times when the world is shaking us, and we don't know what to hold on to. Self-esteem is taking a beating all over the planet. What used to be for us bastions on which our security or stability rested: financial position, job or relationship, can disappear overnight and it is important that our self-esteem is strong in the face of these unforeseen onslaughts of life.

The **Awakening of Consciousness** workshop is aimed at people who are ready to take a step further in their process of evolution and change. Its aim is that the person achieves living in a permanent state of connection and oneness with everything through a change of perception.

The **Path to Meditation** workshop is aimed at both children, adults and executives. During twenty hours, training is offered to turn the habit of meditating into a powerful tool for transformation. Although there are many meditation techniques, the COR Method seeks to show the ways the person can connect with himself, through the way he relates to his emotions, thoughts and senses. The tragedy for all of us is that we have trained ourselves to live permanently in conflict or with an internal struggle. The goal of meditating is that we can increasingly dissolve that inner struggle.

This is a task that requires great vital energy, so it is very important that we focus on the vision of what we want. Keeping courage activated is crucial in the COR Method process. There is no time to waste. The breathtaking pace of the times we live requires us to be focused, to resolve things, and with greater efficiency.

The premise of the COR Method has been to form a system of therapeutic resources to facilitate change and evolution. The challenges of the 21st century that all of humanity is experiencing — uncertainty, isolation, poverty, famine, overpopulation, migratory movements, information overexposure, fake news, the difficulty of discerning true from false, immediacy, climate change, and artificial intelligence, to name just a few — make it imperative to increase our levels of awareness, to provide intelligent and efficient responses as a species, and prevent us from collapsing under circumstances or events that erupt, more often than not, unexpectedly.

The psychological evil of this century is, without a doubt, anxiety in all its manifestations. The constant and vertiginous changes, the feeling of permanent uncertainty in which we live, require robust mental health from us, as well as the capacity for adaptation and flexibility to face all kinds of contingencies. We may have only ten dollars in our bank account, but the only capital we cannot afford to lose is our vital energy. All our therapeutic, psychological and spiritual work is oriented to preserve it and I will never tire of insisting on this. Self-sabotage robs you of energy; low self-esteem robs you of energy. It is urgent that we become aware of this and focus our minds for that purpose.

In this process — from which we therapists and mental health caregivers do not escape either— it is important to become aware of our feelings and emotions and avoid the escapism and dazedness to which we resort to avoid contact with what is affecting us and which only aggravates that feeling of being lost, emptiness and despair.

It is essential to embrace change and not resist it. Humanity is going through one of the most important transitions in our evolutionary process as a species. We are experimenting with a more expanded consciousness, new perceptions of the world and interaction with the environment. Personally, I believe that the ability to change mental programs and patterns is an essential part of our evolutionary work.

Pandemics and natural disasters are the consequence of the irresponsible and excessive use of our planet's resources. The great centers of power are migrating their production structures towards the digital and the green economy. In the social sphere, we are seeing the transformation of societies towards new forms of coexistence, less traditional, but perhaps more inclusive, empathetic and supportive. Obsolete and outdated structures are naturally resisting what threatens their survival, and what we see unfolding before our perplexed gaze is nothing other than the conflict between the old, which resists change, and the new, which struggles to break through.

It has been meaningful for me to reconnect with my roots. In the south of Italy, in a village of only 3500 inhabitants, where my paternal family comes from, I have found a very healing and revealing refuge for aspects that are maturing in me. I have gained a greater understanding of Italy and its culture. This required that I let myself be penetrated by the place and go deeper into that spiritual connection with the land. This was not in my original plans when I left Venezuela. My idea was to stay in Madrid, and this has been one of the many turns that I've had to make because of the pandemic. As a human being, I'm still looking for meanings to guide me, and this is not a closed process. The fundamental thing is that I have been able to continue my vocation of service, supported by the wisdom of my elders and in close harmony with nature, which is my great source of energy and connection with the sacred.

In 2020, of course, my work routine suffered alterations as a consequence of social distancing. Before, I used to take care of my space, meditate, exercise. Previously, with my move to Europe, I had focused on opening paths to the COR Method in other countries. That intensity of change led me to work longer hours. People demanded more in the pandemic and I had to combine schedules from America, Europe and Asia. I am stuck in front of a screen for many hours, and at certain times I have felt overloaded with work. These times, however, have opened in my mind wider spaces of tolerance towards technology. The expansion of sight and hearing tells me how far the amplification of the senses can go. To maintain this rhythm in the best possible conditions, in moments of such intensity, I have increased the frequency with which I participate in silent retreats, whether in person or online.

I had to make some changes to adapt to the new demands of the environment. I also discovered that my body functions much better in cold climates.

Also, because of my own personal process, I was very emotionally overloaded. It has been a very challenging period, but it has helped me to work on myself, which, in the end, is my best tool to treat others. This has made me see my own anxieties, pains, fears, attachments. For a therapist, understanding his or her own humanity is fundamental. This allows them to recognize their personal resources and the ability to see themselves in all their aspects in order to accompany others.

Anxiety, fear, loneliness, and despair are frequent issues that lead people to seek help. It is true that with the pandemic more cases of anxiety have appeared. However, in my opinion, what the pandemic has done is to accelerate or highlight a process in which the whole planet had already been engaged for some years. The number of people with mental illness has increased considerably, and has become a public health problem in many countries.

Before I went to Europe, I had a personal trainer and ate at home. In Spain, thanks to an acupuncturist, I was able to take care of my diet. All this coincided with a period of great suffering: I separated from my partner, emigrated and began to eat very little. My most vulnerable point has always been my stomach. I found it difficult to find balance in the midst of personal turmoil. In addition, I went from living in a house with a garden to a reduced space in a small apartment. A totally abrupt change of life.

In Italy, I let myself get carried away for a while by the local customs, until I decided to take up my own. Since I spend many hours sitting, I need to stretch. I perform *surya namaskar* (the sun salutation) every morning. I also do *kapalabhati* (fast breathing) to increase vital energy or *kundalini**. I drink green juices on an empty stomach and at the moment I am doing a coffee detox and I have replaced it with tea and infusions. I mountain bike and eat smaller amounts. I also do an information detox; I only watch news once a week to stay informed. I'm interested in nature programs, neuroscience and analysis from *The Economist*.

I wake up early in the morning. I feel that this makes me master of my day. I am grateful before going to bed for absolutely everything, the good and the bad. I take good care of my sleep. I do deep meditations before going to sleep and I am grateful for everything I have experienced.

---

* In Hinduism, *Kundalini* is a form of divine feminine energy (or Shakti) believed to be located at the base of the spine, in the muladhara (the root chakra).

All this is a reconquest of my habits and routines that are good for me. I am becoming more and more aware of the importance of maintaining these spaces, because it is very difficult to get all this from the outside world.

Personally, I feel much more confident and that confidence is also felt by the people who come to me.

As for my fears, anxieties and uncertainties, I try to see them, to recognize them and it is in those moments when a confidence emerges that allows me to face them and overcome them. Anxiety sometimes manages to take me over, but I sit down to breathe, I meditate, I talk about it, I don't hide it. When I pay attention to it and don't deny its presence in me, it usually subsides. One of the many things I have reflected on at this stage has been how to achieve a full life and how to reconcile that aspiration with the possibility of not achieving what we dream of, or losing what has been achieved. The answer that comes to me time and again is to remain humble, both in success and failure, and, above all, to foster a state of permanent gratitude for what we have in the present.

The great anxiety of human beings is the fear of death. Much of what we do in our lives hides a fear, sometimes not conscious, of growing old, getting sick or dying. Death is an issue that we must confront and accept as an inevitability that can befall us at any time. It is a fundamental part of the reality principle. We tend to live between guilt for the events of the past and anguish for the future.

The COR Method places our attention on the present moment and the fullness that can only be experienced in it.

Notes

Chapter 1

1. Craniosacral therapy
John Upledger (1932-2012) was an osteopathic physician born in the United States. During a neurosurgical operation to remove a calcium plaque the size of a penny that was attached to the meningeal membrane at the nape of the patient's neck, he was surprised to see the pulsations emitted by the membrane, which did not coincide with the patient's breathing or heartbeat. At that moment Upledger, while helping the neurosurgeon hold the tissues open, could not help but think that possibly the cause of this activity was that the membrane was moving in accordance with the rise and fall of the cerebrospinal fluid.

Based on this observation, Upledger's research showed that the cerebrospinal fluid contained between the meningeal membranes, which cover the brain and the spinal cord, does indeed show a movement that is affected by different situations in each organism. At the same time, the Craniosacral Academy had already concluded that the bones of the skull do indeed move due to the pressure exerted by the cerebrospinal fluid, a hypothesis that had been put forward in 1900 by the osteopath William G. Sutherland.

What followed then was the development of a whole therapeutic method by which, through a subtle manipulation of the areas of the craniosacral system, the different alterations of the fluid can be perceived according to the physical or emotional ailment of the patient. This implied the development of a whole technique to learn to perceive these fluctuations.

> What my hands can feel has become a great source of understanding about many things, including this semi-closed hydraulic system that we would soon call the craniosacral system.

For thirteen years, Upledger taught Biomechanics at the College of Osteopathic Medicine at Michigan State University while leading a team of professional anatomists, biophysicists, physiologists and bioengineers who developed the published research that is the foundation of craniosacral therapy.

In 1985 he created the Upledger Institute International in Palm Beach Gardens, Florida, to train and certify therapists and care for patients. Craniosacral therapy has spread significantly in different countries around the world.

2. Wilhelm Reich (Austro-Hungarian Empire, 1897-United States, 1957). Physician, psychoanalyst, philosopher and academic.

3. Yuval Noah Harari (Israel, 1976). Historian, writer. Professor at the Hebrew University of Jerusalem.

4. Howard Gardner (United States, 1943). Psychologist, researcher and educator, known for his theory of multiple intelligences. https://psicologiaymente.com/inteligencia/teoria-in-teligencias-multiples-gardner

5. Daniel Goleman (United States, 1946). Psychologist, writer and journalist, famous for his studies on emotional intelligence, a theory about which he has written several books.

https://ciec.edu.co/wp-content/uploads/2017/08/La-Inteligencia-Emocional-Daniel-Goleman-1.pdf

Chapter 2

6. Irvin David Yalom (United States, 1931). Psychiatrist and writer. Maximum exponent of existentialist psychology.

Chapter 3

7. Amos Oz (Israel, 1939-2018). Writer and novelist. Goethe Award 2005 and Prince of Asturias Award for Literature 2007.

8. Lynne McTaggart (United States, 1951). Activist, writer, lecturer and journalist. Author of several books on alternative medicine and the relationship between science and spirit.

9. In chapter 4 we refer to the levels of consciousness developed by David R. Hawkins, Ph. R. Hawkins (United States, 1927-2012). Physician and philosopher, professor and writer. Pioneer in research on consciousness. Author of several books that have been translated into different languages.

10. Gestalt therapy

Although Gestalt is known as a current of psychology that began in Germany with thinkers such as Wolfang Köhler, Max Wertheimer and Kurt Koffka, it was not until 1940 that the psychoanalyst, Fritz Perls (also German), developed in the United States, together with his wife, Laura Posner, the entire therapeutic methodology that emerged from this school.

"Gestalt" is a German word that in English translates as 'form' or 'configuration'. Gestalt psychology is based on studies of perception and how in each individual it is produced differently according to his or her own background or memory. Therefore, its fundamental premise, "the whole is more than the sum of its parts", is based on a holistic conception of the human being, who must be explored through his sensory, intellectual, affective and spiritual experiences, in order to understand him as an integral being.

Gestalt therapy uses different resources to help the patient achieve closure in his or her life processes of wounds that have been left open and that condition his or her emotional and physical health. Closing unfinished relationships and learning to forgive are necessary steps for the development of personal self-awareness, which, ultimately, will allow the transformation of suffering, if not happiness, in a state of peace and tranquility.

According to the French psychologist Serge Ginger, "Gestalt does not simply aim to explain the origins of our problems, but to investigate the paths to new solutions [...] It is not a matter of understanding, analyzing or interpreting events, behaviors or feelings, but rather of promoting a global awareness of our way of functioning, of our processes of creative adjustments to the environment, of the integration of the present experience, of our avoidances and of our defense mechanisms (resistances)".

Today it is generically known as "doing Gestalt" to conclude a process or a cycle as a necessary condition to be able to move forward. Authors and therapists agree that Gestalt therapy, beyond a healing treatment, proposes a philosophy; a way of living life.

Source: https://psicologiaymente.com/biografias/fritz-perls-psicologia-gestalt

Chapter 4

11. Cambridge Declaration on Consciousness in Animals and Non-humans.
https://www.animal-ethics.org/declaracion-consciencia-cambridge/

12. David. R. Hawkins (United States, 1927-2012). Physician and philosopher, professor and writer. Pioneer in the investigation on the conscience. Author of several books that have been translated into different languages.

13. Edith Eger (Hungary, 1927). Psychologist and lecturer practicing in the United States. Holocaust survivor. https://dreditheger.com/

14. Brené Brown (United States, 1965). Researcher and lecturer. She has dedicated herself to the study of vulnerability, courage, shame and empathy in people. https://brenebrown.com/

15. Álex Rovira (Spain, 1969). Economist, businessman and lecturer. Author of several essays on values, love and happiness, as well as stories for children. https://www.alexrovira.com/

Chapter 6

16. Blanca Castilla de Cortázar (Spain, 1951). Philosopher and anthropologist. Doctor in Theology. Author of several books on the themes of identity and discourses on gender. https://www.eunsa.es/autor/blanca-castilla-de-cortazar/

Chapter 7

17. Friedrich Nietzsche (Germany, 1844-1900). Philosopher and poet.

Chapter 8

18. Guillermo Feo García (Caracas, 1942). Psychiatrist. Founding director of the Center for Learning and Research in Gestalt Facilitation (*Centro de Aprendizaje e Investigacion en Facilitacion Gestáltica*). Creator and coordinator of training courses in Gestalt theory and practice.

References

Capra, F. (2002). *El punto crucial. Ciencia, sociedad y cultura naciente.* Editorial Troquel.

Feo García, G. (2003). *Caos y congruencia: la terapia gestáltica, un estudio científico de la personalidad.* Editorial Galac.

Germer, C., Siegel, R., & Fulton, P. (2016). *Mindfulness and Psychotherapy.* Guilford Press.

Harari, Y. N. (2016). *Sapiens. De animales a dioses: Una breve historia de la humanidad.* Penguin Random House.

Hawkins, D. R. (2009). *Healing and recovery.* Veritas Publishing.

Lowen, A. (2005). *El lenguaje del cuerpo: dinámica física de la estructura del carácter.* Herder.

McTaggart, L. (2007). *El campo: en busca de la fuerza secreta que mueve el universo.* Editorial Sirio.

Oz, A. (2002). *Contra el fanatismo.* Ediciones Siruela.

Ruiz, M., Fernández, T. and Tamaro, E. (2004). *Biografía de Wilhelm Reich.* Biografías y Vidas. LA enciclopedia biográfica en línea. https://www.biografiasyvidas.com/biografia/r/reich.htm.

Upledger, J. E. (2001). *Craniosacral Therapy Touchstone for Natural Healing.* North Atlantic Books.

Yalom, I. (2010). *La psicología existencial.* Herder Editorial (second edition).

www.ingramcontent.com/pod-product-compliance
Lightning Source LLC
Chambersburg PA
CBHW020415080526
44584CB00014B/1345